CONQUERED FROM WITHIN

A Survivor's Story

by Tom Jelinek

Superare
Dolo
Press

San Diego, CA

CONTENTS

Foreword

This is the true story of a man named Carl. His surname and home village have been withheld at his request, to protect his privacy. Carl was involved in organized opposition to the 1948 communist coup in Czechoslovakia, and for that he was arrested, severely beaten, and sentenced to life as a slave laborer in the country's toxic uranium mines. He owes his survival to a harrowing escape and defection across the highly militarized border with the American Zone of post-war Germany. Carl saw firsthand how systematically Czechoslovakia's institutions were subverted, and how quickly it was transformed from a free country into a Stalinist tyranny. He is still alive and lucid as of this writing, in his late nineties. The author has known Carl for approximately fifteen years, and was given access to Carl's extensive notes, written in the years immediately following the events described, hoping his story would one day be told. This project was undertaken with Carl's full consent and cooperation.

Some background on Czechoslovakia is in order. Today, most remnants of that nation are represented by the independent countries of the Czech Republic and Slovakia. Both nations were part of the Austro-Hungarian empire, which entered the Great War already on the brink of disintegration. Seeing an opportunity carve out an independent nation, future president Tomáš Masaryk spent the war in exile, lobbying the western powers for the creation of the new nation. Masaryk was of both Czech and Slovak ancestry, and argued passionately that the two peoples were one and the same. He was assisted by long-time confidant and later successor, Edvard Beneš. With the end of the war in 1918, the new nation was born. It was composed of Bohemia and Moravia (both considered Czech), Slovakia, and Carpathian Ruthenia in the very east. It was the only state created in the aftermath of the war that maintained a functioning democratic government for the entire duration of the inter-war period, with a prosperous economy to match.

It is not widely appreciated in the west, but the communist coup of February 1948 was vigorously opposed by Prague's students and intellectuals, some 30,000 of whom took to the streets in protest. The demonstrations were orderly and peaceful, but their numbers alarmed the coup plotters. They called in non-governmental communist militias, who descended on Prague armed with Sten assault rifles, and brazenly opened fire on the demonstrators. Many students were killed, and the remainder were tracked down and arrested over the course of the following year. Most were sentenced to short, brutal lives as slave laborers in the country's uranium mines, to provide Stalin with fuel for his atom bomb program. Not many managed to escape. Carl was one of only a few who did, and lived to tell his story. Many of his friends and colleagues did not survive, so this story is dedicated to them.

About the poems: Carl wrote a volume of Czech poems to help him through the process of healing from his emotional wounds. I included a small selection, for their power in getting Carl's story across. In translating them, my priority was fidelity to the themes and feelings expressed over trying to re-create verse structures or rhymes, which is why they seem free-form. They follow traditional poetic conventions in their original Czech.

Introduction

The shove came from nowhere. It impacted my head against the brick wall, and jarred my neck. I felt a surge of anger at whoever it was, but as I prepared to fight back, I caught a glimpse of his face, and my attitude softened. "What's come over you, shoving me like that?"

"They're looking for you, Carl." He was nearly hysterical. "They came by the student residence, ready to take you. Someone's bound to tell them where you're living."

In hindsight, I should have boarded a bus that second, or hitchhiked to the border with the American zone of Germany, and not even returned home for a change of clothes. I had been warned to leave the country several times that summer, and a half dozen people I knew had gone missing. It had become a morbid game, talking about which student, professor, or other university staff member was the latest to disappear. Our eyes had been pried open the previous winter, when they shot dozens of students in the streets of Prague.

But it's no simple thing to uproot your life and leave your home country on the strength of a warning. Even after seeing others suffer. I had just concluded a good summer job, and had begun a graduate program the university. I still clung to the hope of a bright future, and wrestled with the notion that maybe things would not get so bad, or they would not stay bad for very long.

We all knew we needed an escape plan, in case they came after us. My plan was to return home to southern Moravia, bordering Austria. On a recent visit home, an old family friend gave me the usual warning: "Be prepared to get out, fast." But his warning carried more weight than most. He was an officer of the military, responsible for the security of the southern borders, and was very familiar with the power grab in progress throughout the country.

"I'll just come back here," I said, confidently. "I know these lands like the back of my hand. I can hide in the Pálava Hills, or the Ranšpurk forest, and cross the river to Austria in the forested stretches.

He shook his head, compassionately, but insistently. "You're young, Carl. You need to plan for a distant future. Not for two weeks of hiding out. You're talking about spaces no more than a few kilometers across." I was not ready to accept that advice. It was only years later, when I saw the scale of true wilderness in the Canadian north, that I realized how unrealistic my plan was.

With my friend's warning still ringing in my ears, and a sore head from where it bumped the wall, I returned to my apartment thinking it might finally be time to make my way out of Prague. The train stations would be watched, to be sure. But I could not imagine them stopping all commerce, to check everyone's name against their lists.

And what if my friend was exaggerating? Leaving the country would mean interrupting my studies, and maybe losing everything I had worked for. As I was working through my conflicted thoughts, I wandered over to the window, where I saw two large, black cars pulling up in front of my apartment building. Men in ill-fitting overcoats got out of each, and began to talk to each other. *Could they be here for me*? No sooner did I have the thought, than the answer hit me. It was a warm day, so anybody wearing a bulky coat like that was concealing something inside it. Now in a panic, I grabbed my documents, money, and a jacket, and ran down the stairs, hoping it was not too late.

I took the back exit out of the building, hoping to avoid confronting them at the front door. I made my way through the narrow alleyway, out to the street. The top of the street was the only way to get out to the rest of Prague. I stole a quick glance back behind me as I left the alley, and felt like they might be paying attention to me. But I was young and athletic, while they were middle aged, and obviously overweight. I picked up the pace of my walk, reasonably sure they would not be able to keep up.

Feeling intense anxiety, I made my way to the top of the street, where I knew I would be able to blend in with the crowds of Prague. I glanced back again, and noticed one of them was following me on foot, while the other had started his car. My heart began to race as I confirmed I was the target. *If I can get in among the crowds, I'm sure I'll lose them.* Finally, I turned the corner onto the main street, and felt like I had made it. Then something blunt hit me across the face. It may have been a Billy-club, but I don't remember. When I recovered, I was sitting in the back of the car, handcuffed and blindfolded, and feeling pain from the blow I took to the face. The metallic smell of blood was one that would soon become all too familiar.

"Where are you taking me?" I asked, but received no reply.

"Why were you after me?" Again, no reply.

After a few more questions, each of which was ignored, it occurred to me the men probably had no idea why they were instructed to arrest me. I was only a name on a list. I sat quietly for the remainder of the trip, but as my fate was no longer in my hands, I felt strangely relaxed.

The car eventually stopped, and I was pulled out the back, then shoved into a round, damp tunnel, more like a sewer than a corridor. We came to a steel door, which they opened for me, and shoved me inside. There was no light at all, and it was cold and wet. It was only as I tried to move around that I began to bump up against other people. In this crowded cell, nobody was talking, or expressing any emotions at all.

I'm not sure how long I was in the holding cell, but I don't believe it was very long. I had only my thoughts to keep me company, and only just enough time to piece together what happened to me. The secret police at the entrance to my apartment building had indeed come for me, but they were not alone. They had backup at the top of the street, in the man who delivered the blow to my face. After that, it was a simple matter to cuff me, and put me in the car, where I regained my bearings.

Soon, the door opened, and a man's voice read out a list of names in a cold, disinterested manner. My name was among them. We were led to a small room with a little bit of light, where we again waited. It was not long before someone came for me. He took me to a windowless room with a bare light bulb on the ceiling, where three men sat behind a single wooden desk, wearing drab, gray uniforms.

A large man stood behind me, and shoved me down on a small stool. Then the interrogation started.

"We know you were at the treasonous student demonstration."

It seemed pointless to deny it, so I said nothing. I also felt a little numb. I don't think the full gravity of what was happening had sunk in.

The questions then came in quick succession, from all three men, shouting at the tops of their lungs, and exuding contempt with each word.

"Who were your closest associates at school?"

"Who were your associates in the armed forces?"

"What other activities were you involved in?"

After each question, I was dealt a blow with a steel bar, or pipe, directed to the back of my head, and both my shoulders. It seemed to make no difference whether I attempted to speak, as I was never given time to say anything coherent. The next question, and the next blow, swiftly followed the previous. After a while, I gave up trying to answer altogether, and I don't think my interrogators cared, either way.

I don't know how long the interrogation lasted. It felt interminable. I was bleeding from my nose, several places on my head, and both ears. My shoulders and the tops of my arms were badly bruised, and I thought I was as good as dead.

Finally, I was moved to a darker room with six men in the same rough condition as myself. All of us in that room had been badly beaten, and none of us had been given any opportunity to explain ourselves, to ask the purpose of the hearing, the nature of the charges against us, or sentences we might be facing. It was all so pointless, since they did not even listen to anything we tried to say.

I laid down on the wood floor, in a lot of pain. I became nauseous, and dizzy. I could not stop the bleeding from my wounds. After some time, two older women entered, bringing buckets of cold water, and two towels for each prisoner. They washed our faces, cleaned our wounds, and left. We used our shirts to stanch the bleeding after they left.

Once the prisoners had all been interrogated, we were collectively brought before some kind of arbitrator, where we were each presented with a piece of paper with a stamp and signature, stating the outcome of our *trial*. In every case, it read, *life in prison for revolutionary tendencies*. Most of the students, including myself, were specifically sentenced to a life of slave labor in the uranium mines on the western fringe of the country. By this time, the consequences of that sentence were well known. It may have been a life sentence, but it was certain to be a short life, as the conditions in the uranium mines were famously toxic, and the treatment of prisoners, brutal.

That was the beginning of the most difficult period of my life. But in order to properly tell the story, I need to start at the beginning.

Chapter 1: Paradise Lost

I've heard it said that the Garden of Eden was somewhere in Mesopotamia, in modern day Iraq. But I've always believed that to be a mistake. Eden was in southern Moravia, a region in the southwest of today's Czech Republic. At least, that's how I remember it. Between the fields of wheat, the vineyards and fruit trees, the hills presenting their white cliff faces, and the deep mixed forests, it was the perfection of God's creation.

I was born in a village in the middle of Eden, near the border with Austria. We lived in an old house, built by my grandparents, and I was the youngest of three children. I had an older sister and brother, both of whom helped raise me. We had a farm we had worked with our relatives for many generations. It was almost three kilometers' walk from home to the farm, and we made the walk twice a day, separated by a hard day of work. But we took the hard work for granted, and enjoyed every minute of being outdoors in that earthly paradise. From the farm, we had an expansive view of the Pálava Hills, whose forested hills rose above the vineyards to a ruined medieval castle at the top, where artists would gather to paint the endless rows of grapevines, following the gentle curves of the land as they receded into the distance.

My brother was like a second father to me, being ten years my senior. I looked up to him in every way, and he always treated me like a prized child, rather than the nuisance brother I often was. He would walk with me to tend the vineyards, telling me stories along the way, or singing our traditional songs. Sometimes he would pick me up and carry me on his shoulders, and I marveled at the strength of his arms, and the gentleness of his manner. Then, when we arrived at the vineyard and began work, his concern for me would make him occasionally stop his work, and wave to me from a distance, so I would know he was there if I needed him.

> *Our lands were alive with happy people,*
> *Colorful costumes and beautiful song.*
> *Our people full of love for our country,*
> *Anger was foreign to our way of life.*

> *Deep was our love for the land,*
> *The autumn crocus creeping on to country lanes,*
> *Our meadows were expansive bouquets,*
> *Flowers of every color and fragrance.*

> *We danced round the village, singing from the heart,*
> *And our songs were answered by the earth,*
> *Every flower was like a ringing bell*
> *Every blade of grass a harp string.*

> *The joyful harmony of our work and songs,*
> *Heralded the ripening of wheat,*
> *Praising God for the gifts of the earth,*
> *Before the reapers plowed it up.*

Busy as we were, there was still time for sports, and we enjoyed our share. We were taught gymnastics, boxing (at which I later became quite good), archery, and countless other activities. We played soccer any time we could, when our farm work was complete. In winter, we would skate or play hockey, usually on flooded fields. But at times the ice was uneven, or if a thaw came, the fields quickly became unplayable. The ponds held up better, but there was always the danger of breaking through the ice, so our parents forbade us from skating on them. But being young boys, we had our own ideas. At first, the sound of cracking ice sent us scurrying off the pond, but eventually, we decided that sound meant nothing. Then on one occasion, it nearly proved fatal. Several of us set up a game of shinny, where no score is kept, and we simply tried to deliver the puck to a defined spot on the other team's side of the ice. The pops and cracks in the ice were by now familiar, and none of us were overly worried. The competition was intense, but it was interrupted by a loud crack, together with a *plunk*, from the middle of the pond. One of my friends was suddenly under the water. The ice started cracking and popping all over, and I became afraid it would also happen to me, so I skated to the edge of the pond. I had not even reached the shore, when I had a vision of his mother's face, as I struggled to explain to her how he drowned.

I turned around, and saw the stick protruding from the hole in the ice, flailing helplessly. Acting mostly on instinct, I laid down on my stomach and extended my arms and legs, to spread my weight over a larger area. I crawled over to the hole in the ice, and pulled on his stick. It was still in his hand, so I pulled until I got his head and shoulders up above the water. Then the edge of the hole began to give, and I had to back up, but at least he could breathe. He was coughing uncontrollably, probably from inhaling cold water. I waited until his coughing eased, then stretched my stick out to him. He grabbed it, and I backed up slowly, until I managed to pull him out of the water, on to more solid ice. We went straight home, and were all severely scolded for ever going out on that pond.

On festive occasions, the vibrant colors of traditional Czech costumes always signaled an abundance of good food, drink, singing, and dancing. The border with Austria was a short walk, and our Austrian neighbors often joined in our celebrations (and we in theirs). I was not aware of any tension between peoples, and interacting with our neighbors to the south seemed perfectly normal. Most Austrians spoke Czech reasonably well, which made everything easier.

We had whatever we needed and a little extra, but we were still poor by modern standards. The family had a single bicycle, so it was a special treat to be allowed to ride it, as it was normally reserved for farm business. When I was twelve, I was assigned the task of delivering wine and slivovice (a Czech favorite, slivovice is distilled from fermented plums) to shops in nearby Austrian villages. I would load the bicycle with one five liter jug of wine on each side, and a jug of slivovice in my rucksack. The ride to the Austrian village of Reinthal was a gentle downhill cruise, and it was pure joy to glide down that hill with the wind in my hair, especially if any friends came along for the ride. We followed the road through a forested area, then cruised across the border into Austria without even slowing down as we passed the small, unattended border sign by the side of the road. I've been asked whether I was ever tempted to sample the goods, and the answer is no, never. I understood perfectly well that this was our livelihood, and I was responsible for delivering it. Besides, we were allowed a small amount on festive occasions, so I never thought of it as something exotic.

The Pálava Hills, photographed from the west. Vineyards still line the lower slopes, while the ruined castle sits at the very top.

My favorite destination was a shop that stocked wines and baked goods, at the northern edge of Reinthal. I was always greeted by a pretty girl of my age, named Monika. She had big blue eyes, slight dimples in her cheeks, and a warm smile that always made my day. When her parents weren't looking, she would give me a small pastry or other treat, to let me know she enjoyed my visits as much as I did. After delivering our goods, I made the return trip uphill, considerably lighter, smiling and reveling in the perfection of my little corner of the world.

In the fall, I would make a little extra money helping hunters in the surrounding wilderness. My job was to go into the woods and disturb the wild hares, or partridge, which would scatter, and give the hunters a chance to make their shots. But on occasion, the hunt was more serious. Wild boar were a nuisance to farmers, as they would often damage crops, so it was important to keep their numbers under control. But they have large tusks, and are known to occasionally attack people, with gruesome results. One day I joined a hunting party, and was assigned to make my way around to the back side of a forest, make a lot of noise, and flush out any wild boar. It took me a half hour to reach my starting point, and then I started to move back through the forest, watching and listening for boar. A short time later, I heard commotion and shooting in the distance. It appeared the hunting party had found boar, and went off in another direction. I shrugged, and started to make my way back through the forest. Eventually, I reached a clearing near where we started, and sat down with my back to a tree. It was a beautiful fall day, and I had gathered a few wild mushrooms along the way, which I now started to clean, and examine for worms. I was lucky. These were perfect boletes, and my mother would be thrilled to put them in a gravy or soup. But as I finished brushing off evergreen needles, moss, and other forest litter, I heard a grunting sound coming from straight ahead. I knew the sound immediately, and looked up to see a large boar running directly at me. Leaving the mushrooms where they were, I scampered up the tree as far as I could, until I was confident I was out of its reach. It came straight over to my beautiful collection of mushrooms and chewed them up, right in front of me. I shouted at it, waved my arms, and even broke some dry branches off the tree, so I could bang them together, to make more noise. But the boar simply grunted at me, then decided to sit there, at the base of my tree. In a few minutes, it was joined by two more, slightly smaller than the first, but still menacingly large. I was stuck, and any attempt to escape these animals would be futile. If they saw me as any kind of threat, they would certainly skewer me.

The day grew late, and I began to feel drowsy, sitting up in that tree. If I fell asleep, I could fall to the ground and get mauled by the boars. The sun was nearing the horizon, and it would soon be dark. I began to fear the worst, until I heard a party of hunters approaching. I began shouting as loudly as I could, and eventually succeeded at drawing their attention. Seeing me stranded in the tree, they laughed a little, then fired a few shots into the air, and the boars scattered in different directions. I thanked them profusely, and came down from the tree. "Why didn't you shoot the boars?"

"They were too close to you. We couldn't be sure it would be a safe shot."

The hunters shared their food with me, and we all laughed at the day's events, glad that nobody had been hurt. I even found a few more fresh mushrooms on my way home.

By the time I was fifteen, I was devoting more time to school, because although I loved farm life, I had developed a fascination with anything electronic, and wanted to be an engineer. The thought of designing those amazing devices seemed like a dream. But there was still plenty of work in summertime, and as the spring neared, I was excited to return to the farm full time. I continued to visit Monika whenever I could come up with an excuse, and I think she continued to enjoy my attention, too. One Sunday afternoon about the start of April, I began the walk to Reinthal, as the roads were too muddy for the bicycle. Thinking of Monika, I felt like I was walking on air, and began singing my favorite Moravian folk songs. Then, as I cleared the forested area, I glanced up, and froze in my tracks.

There was a military checkpoint on the Austrian side of the border. Two guards stood at the side of the road, each holding some kind of rifle with a large magazine. To the side was an unmanned machine gun nest, and the spaces to the sides were blocked off with coils of barbed wire.

I turned around and ran home, deeply disturbed by the unwelcome sight. I met several people as I ran, and the first group noticed my affect, and asked what was wrong. I explained what I saw, and it also seemed to come as a surprise to them. I slowed down to a regular walk, and soon met an older man I knew, who looked like there was a load on his shoulders.

"Have you seen the border?"

He nodded sadly, and began to describe something called an *Anschluss*. I was only half listening, as upset as I was. He also advised me not to try to cross the border without all sorts of documents I had never heard of, never mind actually having any of them.

"What would they do to me?"

"You'd best not find out. They killed a man last week."

The walls of my world had just tightened around me, as I realized I could no longer cross the border. I thought constantly of Monika and her family, and soon I could think of little else. I became distracted, and even my studies began to suffer. It was May, and soon we would begin to work the fields, leaving us with no spare time. So one Sunday afternoon, I gave in to my instincts. I walked down to a hamlet named Boří Dvůr, that bordered a small but dense forest. Still dressed in my Sunday clothes, I made my way through the forest, many times snagging my knit jacket on twigs. Each time, I quickly stretched the fabric, trying to retract the protruding loop, and prevent serious damage. I was only partially successful. The density of the forest meant the authorities had not paid much attention to the borderline where forest met farmland. Or so I thought, at the time. The field was very muddy, and I soon realized I was ruining my shoes. I took them off and carried them, walking barefoot through cold mud.

I was a hundred meters from the road, and felt like I was making good progress, but then I saw a large black car approaching. No ordinary person in these parts owned a large car. It could only be the Nazis, and my German was not nearly strong enough to pass for an Austrian. I was seized by panic, knowing I had no defense if I was spotted. The car was nearing, and I was sure the occupants could see me by now. I was in a low section of the field, so I fell flat on my stomach, face down in the mud. My clothes would certainly be ruined, but that was the least of my concerns. The car slowed, as if someone was scanning the area. Then it stopped, and a soldier with a rifle emerged. I tried my best to avoid even breathing, and prayed he would not see me there, poorly camouflaged by the contour of the land and stubble in the field, left over from last year's crop.

I dared not even look up, hoping against hope that the soldier was only scanning the forest line. Then the soldier returned to the car, and spoke into a radio. I could not make out what he was saying, but the tone of his voice dropped at the end of each phrase. He seemed to be reporting a negative outcome of a search. But what were they searching for?

The soldier listened to the radio for a moment longer, answered with a *nein*, shrugged, and drove off. Only then did I dare exhale. I got up, and saw I was covered with mud from head to toe. I found some water in a ditch at the side of the road, and rinsed off the worst of the mud. I was thoroughly soaked through, in any case. I walked along the road, approaching Reinthal from the west. It was silent, and I was sure I could hear any car approaching from quite a distance. I skirted the village to the north, and made my way to Monika's family's shop. Slowly, I regained my nerve, and was truly excited to see her again, regardless of my appearance. I turned the corner, and was about to enter the shop, when the sight hit me as abruptly as a hockey stick to the teeth: The large black car, parked on the street directly in front of the shop.

I might have stood in front of the shop for several minutes. I had no idea what to do next. Then I heard an old woman's voice behind me, speaking in broken Czech. "You, come over here." Turning, I recognized the woman as a neighbor I had greeted many times over the years. "Quickly, before they see you," she said, sounding irritated by my slow grasp of the situation.

"I came to see Monika," I said as I approached the woman. She was uninterested in my purpose, but grabbed the soaking lapel of my coat with more strength than I thought her capable of, and pulled me inside her house.

"Can't you see? They've been evicted. The Nazis live there now."

"Evicted?" I asked in surprise. "Why?" I was trying to imagine what technicality of the law they might have violated, but the woman cut me off.

"Because they had a convenient house, near the border. It's their field headquarters, now."

"What about the family?" I asked with concern.

She shook her head, and said, "They moved to Vienna. They have relatives there."

I said nothing, as I tried to wrap my head around the implications. Monika was farther away than I could possibly hope to travel. I was suddenly unsure how I would even manage to get home, given my close call in the field. As if sensing my thoughts, the woman said, "You need to get back across the border, before they find you. I've heard them bragging over there, about shooting Czechs."

"They almost found me on my way down. It seemed like they expected someone to be there."

She shook her head in frustration over what I guessed she saw as my stupidity. "They have trip wires all along the border. But they get a lot of false alarms, with deer, boar, and dogs."

It then dawned on me that the soldier I saw was responding to an alarm, and announcing on the radio that he had found nothing. I was lucky. "I'll cross the same field as before, and by the time they respond to any alarm, I'll be back home."

She shook her head with an expression that said, *Don't be an idiot, boy.* "If you tripped a line, there will be more frequent patrols. They'll shoot you on sight, if they don't know you to be the farmer of that field."

"What should I do, then?"

"Have a seat by the fire, and dry out your clothes, for starters." She made me some hot tea, and hung my wet clothes by the fire. She then put on her headscarf, and said, "I'll be back soon. I have an idea."

I watched her through the window, as she walked past Monika's shop. Two Nazi officers were standing outside, and said something to her as she passed. She gave them a dismissive wave, and shook her head. They laughed, and paid her no further attention. She walked down the street a ways, then knocked on a door.

While she was gone, I was overwhelmed by a feeling of despair. In all my youth, people never harmed each other. At least not seriously. Even the odd fight was invariably followed by some form of reconciliation. The community would not stand for anything else. But what power did the community have, when faced with these ruthless foreigners?

She returned in short order, and barked instructions at me. "Franz is taking a wagon of hay over to Bernhardsthal."

I knew right away what she was getting at. Bernhardsthal was close to the river, where the ground is marshy, and the Germans could not patrol as extensively. I would follow the river back home.

We waited until the black car pulled away, and Franz came by with his horse-drawn cart. I climbed into the hay pile without slowing the cart in the slightest, and we were off. The smell of hay was familiar, and I soon felt relaxed. It was also pleasantly warm, deep in the hay, with dry clothes. The ride to Bernhardsthal went by quickly enough, but then the cart stopped abruptly, and I heard someone barking orders in German. Franz named the farm he was going to, while the German walked around the cart. I shrunk back into the hay as deep as I could, and listened. Hay was rustling around me, as something was repeatedly poked into it. And then he barked a command, at which the cart began to move once again. We rode for another few minutes, and I occasionally heard some commotion that I took for everyday activity in Bernhardsthal. Then the

24

commotion died down, and Franz shouted a greeting. The greeting was returned from a distance, and I realized we were at our destination. "The ride ends here," he said quietly, in my direction. "The river is to the east."

The sun was now descending into the west, so it was a simple matter to orient myself. I quickly located the line of trees at the edge of the river, thanked Franz, and ran off. I heard him conversing with the farmer as I went, and I think they were talking about me with some amusement. I made my way through several fields, stepping in more mud, and even cow droppings. I crossed a road, then ran through more fields, nearing the River Thaya, when I heard the sound of rifle shots. "Halt," someone shouted.

The tree line was tantalizingly close, so there was no way I was going to halt. I ran as fast as my young legs would carry me, towards the trees. Another round of shots was fired, and I heard several hitting the trees ahead of me. These shots were no longer being directed into the air.

I entered the forest, but did not slow down. The leaves had not yet grown in, so I could not count on them for cover. But I was confident I could out-run any German soldier, carrying his heavy weapon. That confidence was shattered when I heard the barking of dogs, coming from the same direction. The river was just ahead, but the dogs were gaining on me. My plan to follow the river upstream was now moot; I would have to cross the river. It was not overly deep, but I could not afford to wade through slowly. With the dogs now only a stone's throw behind me, I ran straight into the river, and swam as fast as I could. The water was still cold, but I did not care. It was maybe twenty meters across, but it seemed to take forever. I imagined the dogs swimming after me, or the soldier catching up and shooting me. On reaching the opposite bank, I burst out of the water, and again ran as fast as I could. My lungs were burning, and I was desperately cold, but I did not slow down.

Only after reaching the tree line did I briefly turn, to see the dogs had not crossed the river. The soldier reached the river, and raised his weapon. I turned and ran, hearing more shots fired into the trees. Several bullets passed close enough for me to hear them whistling through the air, while others hit branches and tree trunks. I kept moving as fast as I could. Soon I was in a clearing, and saw buildings ahead. Another few steps, and I was sure there were soldiers ahead, and heavy weaponry. I started to panic, fearing I had failed to cross the border, when it dawned on me that the building was flying a Czechoslovak flag. It was Fort Pohansko, being fortified to defend us against the German threat.

The soldiers soon noticed me, and stepped forward to investigate. I raised my hands, and through my heavy breathing, managed to say, "I'm Czech. The Germans were shooting at me."

The front soldier lifted his weapon up into the air, which I took as a signal that it was okay to approach. "Let's go this way," he said, and directed me past a small pond. There, I passed a concrete bunker, surrounded by heavy artillery.

"You're getting ready?" I asked.

"We *are* ready," he replied, with an expression of defiance.

He took me to the officer in charge, and I was asked all manner of questions. They soon accepted that I was who I said I was, but the questions continued, about what I had observed of German forces. They were lightly armed, by my estimate. They could kill individual people trying to cross the border, or terrorize the farmers, but posed no threat to the fortifications on our side. After questioning, the soldiers gave me a change of clothes and a cup of hot tea, then sent me on my way home. It was already after dark, but I assured them I knew the way perfectly well.

One of the fortifications at Fort Pohansko. It remains in place today, as part of a museum.

It was only as I approached home that I began to worry about my parents' reaction to my misadventure. But I was met with a warm embrace from my mother, and a few sobs. They knew where I had gone the moment I was not accounted for. And they were terrified of what might have happened to me.

I never saw Monika again. I've often thought of her, and what might have happened to her during the war, but those concerns would soon be replaced by more pressing ones.

Summer arrived and work began on the farm, but the joy that used to fill our days had vanished. It seemed like everyone was on edge, as though aware of an imminent danger they were afraid to discuss openly. Then came one Saturday night, late in the summer of 1938, when a vicious storm ripped through the countryside, and toppled several old trees. The house shook as though there had been an earthquake, and I did not get much sleep. The following morning, I joined a lively group of visitors that often assembled at our house on Sunday mornings, before we all went to church. My mother would make coffee or tea for everyone, and the discussions were always fascinating to me. At first, I thought they were discussing the storm, but soon realized the subject was something far more ominous: Gathering storm clouds, coming from Germany.

"Carl, glad you're here," said my father. "We're afraid that at your age, it might not be safe for you to stay here, so close to the border."

"Why not?" I asked, but my question was ignored. My uncle was among the visitors that day, which was a rare treat, as he now lived in Prague. As I sat down and joined him, he said, "Your father told me about your interest in electronics. How would you like to come to Prague, to attend a specialized technical school?"

"And live with you?"

"Sure. I live close enough to the school."

I knew it was a perfect opportunity, and I had always been close to my uncle. But I also knew it would come at the cost of leaving the farm I loved so deeply. That's when my brother, who always seemed to know what I was thinking, said, "Carl, you should go. I can take care of things here, and besides, your destiny lies elsewhere."

I gave him a sad look, and he seemed to understand my mixed feelings. As he put his hand on my shoulder, the melancholy look seemed to say everything. He was happy for me, but he seemed to understand we would not be a part of each others' lives anymore.

It did not take long to make my decision. The age of Eden never lasts forever, and by now, I had the sense that our world was about to be turned upside down. But there was no way I could have imagined the inhuman ferocity that was to come.

Chapter 2: Prague During the War

It did not take long for the conversation to return to Hitler's intentions for Czechoslovakia. One of our guests was Jan, who as a rising officer in the Czechoslovak armed forces, had information the rest of us had no hope of accessing. "The moment he secured the Austrian Anschluss, his attention turned entirely to us."

"We're allies of France," objected my uncle. "He wouldn't dare come after us, and risk war with France, would he?"

Jan looked at my uncle with a sour smile, and said, "We don't think the French will help us."

"Then what's the use of the alliance?" objected Zdenek, a portly old neighbor.

"The French hoped it would deter another trench war with Germany," explained Jan, patiently filling us in. "But France is a shadow of its former glory. They're missing a whole generation of their bravest men."

"What are they left with? Cowards?" asked Zdenek, frowning.

Jan shrugged, as though the question were irrelevant. "The French exhausted themselves defending their country. I don't see us doing the same."

I was at first reluctant to weigh in on the matter, considering myself no match for the wisdom of my elders. But having seen our defenses in person, the question began to burn on my tongue, so I spoke up. "We're not cowards. We're well armed, and ready. Why don't we stand up to Hitler?"

There was an uncomfortable silence, before Jan answered. "That's been talked about a lot, Carl. And for what it's worth, Hitler is afraid of our weaponry, and our fortifications."

"I knew it. I'd gladly fight for our side."

Jan only smiled at me, and seemed to hope the issue would go away. But my uncle's interest had been aroused. "If Hitler is afraid of us, why are we even talking about this?"

Jan sighed, as though he would rather not answer. He glanced around the table, and seemed to accept that he owed his friends the full truth. "The President won't fight without international support, and it doesn't look like anyone is in the mood for war."

I did not like his explanation at all. "Who in their right mind would fight for a nation unwilling to fight for itself?"

"That may be our undoing."

"Then what are we supposed to do?" I asked, frustrated.

"Our choices are to fight alone, or accommodate Germany's demands."

"What demands?" asked my uncle.

"Hitler's demanding the Sudetenland, and our allies want us to surrender it."

"Surrender?" asked my uncle, furious with the answer. "That's our only line of defense."

Jan nodded in agreement, as there was no denying the obvious: The borders of Czechoslovakia followed mountains and rivers, and were easy to fortify. But behind those fortifications was flat ground that could not easily be defended.

"What if he wants more, after that?" asked my uncle.

"After that, he can take whatever he wants," said

Jan, with resignation.

The silence was interrupted by the crashing of a tray to the floor, the breaking of cups and saucers, and the spilling of coffee. Ordinarily, everyone would get up and help clean up, but on that day, hardly anyone paid attention. Far weightier was the realization that we were might surrender without firing a shot.

On the train to Prague, I struck up another conversation with my uncle, still unhappy with the explanations I had heard. "I saw our fortifications down at Fort Pohansko. I spoke with some of the soldiers. They're eager to fight."

"I know what you're saying," he replied, without any life in his voice. "But this country was cobbled together from too many different nationalities."

"You think our own soldiers would turn on us?"

"It's not what I think that matters. It's what our leaders believe. And we have other problems, besides Hitler. The Slovaks want their own nation. The Hungarians want a slice of the country, and could call on their people. The Poles have a claim against Tešin, and Stalin wants Carpathian Ruthenia."

"But we have superior arms," I protested.

"Agreed. But if we're not a cohesive nation, we have no chance."

A well-spoken man sitting across from us heard the conversation, and chimed in. "When Hitler looks at Czechoslovakia, he sees a wealthy, well-armed nation on his border, allied with the French and Soviets. It's obviously a threat, and the restive German minority gives him a perfect opening."

"An opening for what? He's not stronger than us," I objected.

"That may be true. But he knows Europe wants to avoid war at all costs. He's betting they'll force us to capitulate, like the Austrians."

"What Europe should fear most is German ownership of our arms industry," said my uncle.

"I'm afraid they don't think that far ahead," said the stranger.

The Munich Agreement, and its Aftermath

Czechoslovakia had mutual-defense alliances with France, England, and the Soviet Union, but what form any assistance would take was never defined. It was geographically impossible for the French or English to send forces to landlocked Czechoslovakia. Their only option would have been to start a European war of interlocking alliances, similar to the first World War. That memory was too fresh, and the option was never seriously considered. Not sharing a border with Germany, the English quickly came to understand that they could do nothing of substance to help, while the Czechoslovak government relied excessively on the threat of a wider war to deter Hitler. In reality, that fear only seemed to deter England and France. In a desperate bid to avoid that broader war, English and French leaders met their German and Italian counterparts in Munich. Hitler promised the Sudetenland would be his last territorial claim, and the allies took his promise at face value, signing the Munich Agreement on September 30, 1938. Czechoslovakia was then told it would have to surrender the Sudetenland to Germany, or stand alone in any war that followed.

A Czechoslovak war against Germany would have been difficult, despite sophisticated Czechoslovak armaments. One side was fanatical and ethnically united, while the other was the creation of diplomacy, and surrounded by neighbors with territorial grievances. The French later said the Czechoslovak government was looking for an excuse to surrender, although the Beneš government disputed that claim. Beneš for his part despairingly called Moscow, complaining that the choices being presented were surrender or standing alone in a war with Germany. The Soviets fell back on the wording of their agreement, stating that the alliance would only come into play if the French did their part. Exhausting diplomatic options, Beneš capitulated to Hitler's demands, saying in 1944 that the Polish territorial demand for Tešin is what pushed him over the edge. We cannot be sure if he was inclined to that choice from the beginning, but Hitler certainly exploited his unwillingness to fight.

Czechoslovakia ceded its mountainous borders to Germany, leaving the rest of the country entirely undefended. Seeing his opportunity, Hitler quickly occupied and dismembered Czechoslovakia, in the process capturing intact all Czechoslovak armaments, and military industrial capacity.

Prague During the War

Prague saw a Nazi presence by the spring of 1939, leading to all sorts of new laws and restrictions on everyday life. The Czech language disappeared from radio broadcasts, which were now only in German. But we were not initially subjected to much violence, so we tried our best to continue with our lives. I completed my year at the technical school, gaining me acceptance at the University for the fall semester. Prague also had an organized hockey league, always looking for skilled players. My skating skills were developed mostly playing a free form game back home, so it took me a while to learn the nuances of an organized team game. But once I did, I quickly came to play at a very competitive level, in a city-wide league. As enjoyable as it was to combine school with sports, it was soon disrupted.

In November of 1939, the Nazis broke up a student demonstration, and killed one of its leaders. The funeral attracted very large crowds, and people soon began to voice their displeasure with the German occupation. In response, occupying authorities ordered the closure of all universities, and some 1,200 students ended up in concentration camps. I was new enough at the University that I had not connected with any student movements, so I was not targeted, but my studies came to an abrupt end. And I soon became very homesick. I asked my uncle if I could return home to Moravia and the farm. His answer deflated me. "Carl, the border regions have been annexed by Germany. The village is no longer part of our country."

"What about my family?" I asked.

There was silence, as he raised his resolve. "I'm afraid they've been evicted, and the house has been bulldozed. Your family are staying with relatives."

I don't think I said anything to my uncle, who was obviously struggling to keep his composure as he broke the news. I excused myself and walked along the river, grasping at emotional straws. That house was a fixture in our family, and we always knew it would be there, ready to greet whatever relative turned up. And they bulldozed it, unceremoniously. The thought of my mother, tears flowing over the loss of her home, was crushing. But the sadness quickly gave way to an anger I had never felt before, but would come to feel all too often during the war. I had been raised to forgive, and love my enemies, but my experience was mostly confined to forgiving children who broke the rules of our games. Never before had I confronted such a faceless evil, that had no regard for what their actions did to people.

I dreamed of home more frequently after that. I imagined the flowers in the fields, the fragrance of lilac in spring, and moss in the forest. I no longer cared about getting an education in Prague, which was not happening in any case. All I wanted was to be back on the farm; to return to those glorious days of my youth. And whenever nostalgia softened me up, the demons of hatred followed close behind. I knew we should have fought the Germans tooth and nail. What were we afraid of? I would have gladly given my life, if others could go on living the way God intended us to.

Wave after wave, they drowned our nation,
We met them with sullen faces, wearing everything we
owned,
No longer proud; our spirits broken.
We trod roads paved with pain,
Our heads bowed beneath a sky of gray.

Our countenances furrowed at those killers,
Speechless, with clenched fists, we confronted our
fate,
Stifling our words, fearing unknown ears.
This was the legacy of Nazi terror.

Our songs fell silent, our laughter forgotten,
Everywhere tears, streaming down sunken cheeks.
We stumbled through the wreckage of Eden
Down country lanes, to unknown places

Prague During the War

With heavy hearts we yielded our land,
Terrorized by thunderous tanks and guns,
Shrinking, as foreigners dealt death at every turn.
And from that fear emerged a new nation,
One which forgot how to defend herself.

A thousand years we'd farmed these lands,
Yet now like slaves we skulked before those butchers.
Yet surely the spark of faith survives in our people,
And the nation can be reborn from its destruction.

The universities remained closed for the duration of the war, but we soon found a loophole that allowed many of us to continue our studies. University level courses were soon taught at small schools that were exempt from the rules. I finished my studies in 1942 and was assigned a job with Škoda, whose car and truck business was forced to convert to military vehicles, to support the Nazis' war effort. That knowledge made me quite resentful, but the older workers soon showed me ingenious ways they built *defects* into their vehicles. They cautioned that it was only to be done sparingly, or people would be executed. But it always made my day when we were able to deliver a defective vehicle. I imagined it breaking down in the middle of a battle, and holding up a whole column.

I also found distraction in the company of my hockey teammates, and in those years I came to live entirely for our next game, or practice. We would always tease each other in a good-natured way, and laugh at everything, regardless how serious. For a while, it felt like the problems of the world could not reach us. In summers, I joined a rowing team, training and competing on the Vltava River. But the hockey season was always the happiest time for me. In 1942, we won the city championship. After one of our games, I was introduced to the most famous young Czech hockey player at that time, Jaroslav (Jarda) Drobný. He was scarcely two years my senior but was already a legend. Not only was he an emerging hockey star, he was also a tennis prodigy, having competed at Wimbledon before the war. He came to all the rest of our games, and always stopped to exchange a few pleasant words with me. Unlike most of our colleagues, we were both from poor families, and his roots were also in Moravia, so I assumed he felt some sort of solidarity with me. Then after we won the championship, he surprised me by asking whether I would join his team for the following season. First Czech LTC was one of two perennial contenders for the best team in the country, and Drobný was its premier player. I was flattered, and gladly accepted.

The war seemed to be passing uneventfully from my perspective, although we were all uncomfortably aware that some were being deported to concentration camps. I was in a routine, I had good friends, and mostly avoided thinking about problems back home. I tried my best to avoid any thoughts of the Nazi occupation, and eventually, I would occasionally find myself feeling joy again. Like most people, we secretly listened to news broadcasts from the West, and it was encouraging to hear how the German and Western versions of the same events changed over time. At the beginning of the war, news from both sides seemed relatively objective. Similar facts were reported, from different perspectives. The German side was successful and boasted of it, while the West warned of the same. But as the tide turned in the

East, the German broadcasts became increasingly selective with their facts. We learned to see the holes in the story from those things that should have been mentioned, but were not. Hearing the Western perspective quickly clarified why those holes existed: The Germans were losing to the Soviet Union. However, listening to broadcasts from London was not as simple as changing the station on the radio. All radios were required to have those frequencies disabled, and bear a certification sticker to that effect. But I quickly learned to tweak the radio so it would pick up the London frequency, and could switch it back at a moment's notice.

The Germans generally left us alone to play sports, although our coaches were required to report to them. We always assumed they had to give an accounting of our activities, and whether there was anything subversive going on. As a result, the players and coaches developed an aloofness to each other, so nothing would be said or heard that would have to be reported. And there were always about three uniformed Nazis sitting right behind the players at games. They never interfered, and I don't know if they took any interest in the game, but their presence was an unmistakable reminder that we were always under scrutiny.

I played hockey for First Czech LTC in the winter of '42-'43, but soon found the team was very deep in talent, to the extent that I would only occasionally get to play in games. When I did, I played on Drobný's line and I enjoyed that, but I soon decided I'd rather play regularly, on one of the lesser teams. Jarda understood perfectly when I told him during the off-season that I would join Sparta Prague for the following season. We were never paid for our play, but we traveled throughout the country, and the host team's supporters would usually give us extra food. Our rations were otherwise meager, so it was always welcomed.

Things changed for us after the allies arranged the assassination of Reinhard Heydrich. Reprisals against the Czech people were swift, and thousands were executed in the months that followed, giving us a taste of Nazi brutality. Even after things settled down somewhat, we lived with the constant threat of arrest, deportation to a concentration camp, or outright execution. One winter day, as I walked along the river, an older man in front of me reached into his overcoat, pulled out a handgun, and tossed it into the river. He turned around, and when he saw me, I could tell he was horrified.

Trying to assure him, I said "dobrý den" (good day), so he would know I was Czech.

He exhaled with relief, and as if to justify himself, whispered, "I used to serve in the army, so I had a sidearm. But if they ever found it, I'd be dead."

It would occasionally strike me how sad it was that we had grown accustomed to living under terror. To cope with our situation, we would convince ourselves that nothing would happen to us, personally. When reports reached our ears of someone being arrested, or disappearing, we would forget it as quickly as we could, and move on with other concerns. I think most of us were dealing with one grievance or another that we could openly discuss, lest we say the wrong thing, to the wrong person. But for me, that life of pretending came to an end one day late in 1943. A letter came from home, and as I read it, my heart fell out of my chest. My beloved brother had disappeared. I understood perfectly what that meant: He would never be seen again, and there would be no further information on his fate. He was everything I ever wanted to be. Any time I had felt lonely away from home, I imagined telling him about everything I had been doing, and in my imagination, he always listened approvingly. I always thought I'd soon see him again, so I was constantly anticipating our reunion and rehearsing what I would say. And now he was gone.

The bitterness returned, stronger than ever. Before long, I was consumed with hatred for those animals, lacking a shred of human compassion, and it was eating me up inside.

Remember the indignity of our capitulation,
And all the misery it spawned.
The sufferings of our martyrs,
The blood of our saints, spilled without remorse.

Allow yourselves no time for pleasure,
For our day of vengeance nears!
Woe to him whose hand is soft
And cannot clench into a fist!

Remember how they took your homes,
And blithely killed your sons.
Remember the bitter years,
When you were exiled in your own land,
Answer them with words as sharp as swords!

Bloody were the seeds the Nazis sowed
Bloody also will their harvest be!
My people - avenge your dead, save your living!
My dear people - never forget what they've done
to us!

After that, I could no longer imagine I was speaking with my brother, because it would only remind me that he was gone. At times, I would hope against experience that he was only in prison somewhere, and would eventually be released. But I could not seriously delude myself. The Nazis were nothing if not efficient in matters of death. And I was sickened by the blackness of the thoughts and feelings I now entertained. The sight of the Swastika, the black, orange and white color scheme, and the sound of spoken German would always submerge my soul into a caustic bile. It began to fester inside me, and in place of those quiet moments when I used to find peace thinking of my brother, I imagined his killers meeting with horrible deaths. And in my inability to forgive, I came to hate the Nazis even more for what they had turned me into: An embittered shell of my former self. I retained my smile on the outside, but when I looked inward, I saw an ugly picture, completely at odds with who I used to be.

So when in March of 1945, communists began circulating leaflets calling for an insurrection against the Germans, I felt a strong temptation to join in. I think it was only my revulsion at the crimes the communists had already committed against their own people that kept me at bay.

The Germans were well aware of what was afoot. They were in retreat on both fronts, and with good reason, feared for the safety of their soldiers and civilians. They threatened to destroy the city if they met with any resistance. Then in May, as the American Third Army approached the suburbs of Prague from the west, and the Soviets approached from the east, Prague finally got a taste of war. It began with simple acts of defiance, where Nazi bans against use of the Czech language on radio were flouted, while the civil service began disobeying German ordinances. These small acts were seen as signals, and by noon the next day, groups of German soldiers had been attacked, while others fired into crowds. German soldiers attempted to shut down the radio station, which stayed on the air, and called out for help. In response, Czech police rallied to defend the building, and hearing of the battle in progress, young men began to seize what weapons they could, and arrest Germans. In retribution, snipers on rooftops began to shoot at anybody caught outside.

By the end of the day, armed elements of resistance had captured the telephone exchange, and cut off German lines of communication. Resistance gained control of the city east of the river, most bridges, and the train station. But units of the Waffen SS, retreating ahead of Soviet forces in the east, were now summoned to fight the Prague uprising. To the west, a unit of former Soviet troops that had defected to the German side with the intent of fighting Stalin now turned against Germany, and prepared to fight the Waffen SS in Prague.

It was an electric time to be a young man in Prague. All the anger we had bottled up during the war was looking for an outlet, and it seemed like the time might be upon us. Radio broadcasts kept us informed of the progress of arriving forces, so that night I joined many thousands of others as we labored through the night to construct barriers, intended to keep the Waffen SS at bay. Across the city, we had built some 1,600 barriers by morning. Seeing our defiance, the Germans ordered the firebombing of the city, hitting the radio building, many of our barriers, and residential buildings. Casualties were relatively heavy, for what was a brief raid. I later learned that the extent of the firebombing was severely limited by a German lack of fuel, which was needed for their retreat.

Over the next day, the Waffen SS captured the train station, which then became the scene of fierce fighting, resulting in its recapture by Czech resistance. There were sporadic reports of a ceasefire, but the fighting seemed to continue, regardless. I helped with logistics every night, as the factories were now closed in any case. And slowly, the Nazis began to leave Prague, preferring to surrender to the Americans in the west, over the approaching Soviets. I began to resent the possibility that those murderers could avoid their due punishment by fleeing to American forces, who would treat them in accordance with all the protections of the Geneva Convention.

The situation in the streets changed in a hurry. At first, we cautiously ventured out at night, to work on our barriers. But as the retreating German forces lost their intimidating edge and took flight, our people responded like packs of wild dogs, seeing their prey turn and run. I walked through the city, not sure what I wanted to see or accomplish, but I felt compelled to be there for those events. And what I saw changed me. The Waffen SS executed many as discipline broke down, and often used women and children as human shields throughout the fighting, casually killing them when they were no longer needed. Many of their bodies were later found mutilated.

As enraged as I was to see the evidence of such war crimes, I was even more disgusted by what history might consider the *lesser* crimes of my own people. Many captured German soldiers were murdered, often in grisly fashion. Their bodies were left in the open for all to see. A close friend hysterically recounted how sickened he was by the sight of an older Czech woman tending a fire, over which she was roasting a dead German soldier, and carving Swastikas into the corpse. Many German civilians were the targets of violence, officially encouraged by the Czech government in exile, in an attempt to force them flee the country. And once mobs of formerly oppressed people ruled the streets, the violence was not discriminating. Sometimes it was directed against German civilians, but other times open murder was used to settle grudges between neighbors. Still others simply treated that period of anarchy as an excuse to rape and pillage.

As I saw things deteriorate, and heard the stories of Czech war crimes, I began to imagine the whole picture as a mirror, in which I could clearly see my reflection. When those events began, I openly embraced the fantasy that one of the dead German soldiers may have been the one who killed my brother. But I soon began to see my own instincts at work in the various war crimes. The acts were revolting, and made me feel physically sick, but on the other hand, I had to ask myself: *In their shoes, would I have done different*? And as I saw the other side suffer, my hatred for the Germans dissipated. Circumstances dictated who was the victim, and who was the criminal. Turn the tables, and the victims were perfectly capable of becoming the criminals. By the time it was over, I saw the Germans as victims of the culture of war, just as we were. As I began to relate to them as people, I was finally able to pronounce the words that had eluded me for a year and a half: *I forgive*. In that moment, I felt the ugly presence inside me leave, and felt inner peace for the first time in years.

I remember being certain that if we had fought the Germans with that kind of ferocity in 1938, there might not have been an actual second world war. But as it played out, the war left our people with the sense that inhuman acts could be employed in the service of a worthy objective. The Germans did it to us, so we felt justified doing it to them. And those who morally degraded themselves this way would prove very useful the new regime, scarcely three years later.

Chapter 3: Lead-Up to the Coup

Prague was briefly occupied by Soviet troops, consisting mostly of Russians who gave little indication of familiarity with civilized conduct. The Germans were often inhumanly brutal, but their brutality was a tactic, meted out to achieve their stated goals. There was a discipline to their evil that the Russians lacked entirely. The crimes committed by the Russians seemed to stem from ignorance, rather than malice. A Russian soldier might steal a motorcycle from one resident of Prague, use it for some time, then give it to another resident, chosen at random. They were also fascinated with wrist watches. Most soldiers wore several watches at any given time, and would give them away to random people as readily as they stole them. I don't think it was avarice, as much as a disregard for the rules of ownership, where it's understood that people have to save money to buy something valuable, giving them an exclusive claim to that object. Less quaint was their disregard for the rights of our women, who were afraid to walk outdoors, so brazen were Soviet soldiers about kidnapping and rape. One might think it normal for an occupying army, but the Americans who occupied the western portion of the country received few complaints. In any event, we were only too glad when the Soviets left, a short time later.

Before the Soviet withdrawal from Prague was even complete, I was notified that my mother was ill, and might not last long. I left for Moravia right away, but I arrived too late. My father said the grief over losing her son had devastated her, and she never recovered. My absence while she faced her grief weighed heavily on me. The evil deeds of the Nazis were having secondary effects, and I experienced the full range of emotions all over again. I went off on my own, and cried inconsolably for hours. Everything that was good and beautiful about being back home now felt somehow defiled. It occurred to me that those of us who survived would never again be able to enjoy the beauty of the land, or the fragrance of a flower, like we used to.

I was not long at home when I received notice that I had been drafted to serve in the newly re-formed Czechoslovak military. I made an appointment to plead my case, because my father was very vulnerable at that time, and needed me around. The officer listened politely, but was not moved. "There were a lot of tragedies during the war. If we gave everyone a deferral, we wouldn't be able to raise an army."

I quickly learned the reason for the rush: Stalin's troops withdrew from most of Czechoslovakia, but remained in the easternmost province of Ruthenia, which he later annexed to the Ukraine. If we stood any chance of withstanding his threats, we needed to re-arm in a hurry.

The military reviewed my education, and quickly assigned me to a technical unit responsible for deploying pulsed Doppler radar systems that would play a key role in our future air defenses. I took to the technology right away, and was fortunate to be stationed near home, where I could see my father on occasion. Normality began to creep back into my life, and while I often experienced dark periods of sorrow and anger, I consoled myself that at least I was doing my part to prevent it from happening to our nation again.

Not long after I settled in with my unit, our leaders realized that our radar systems were unsophisticated, and would need serious upgrades to match the best Western systems. I understood that to play a significant role in their development, I would have to return to school, and earn a graduate degree. And that meant a return to Prague. As I began the lengthy process of getting permission to transfer, I was paid an unexpected visit from three of my hockey friends: Jarda Drobný, Vlado Dobr, and Standa Konipašek. I felt overjoyed that they took the trouble to come and visit me, while they were in the area. We relived old times, and spoke with real optimism about our future, with the country again run by our own leaders. I think we all expected a return to something like the golden age between wars. Then Jarda said, "We'd like to rekindle the hockey league in Prague, and hope you can join."

I explained that I was already working on a transfer, and would be delighted to play in Prague again. "But are you going to be there? Rumor has it the NHL is interested in you."

"I'm staying," he replied, emphatically. "This is my home. Anyway, I need to my maintain amateur status, if I want to continue to play tennis on the world stage."

I agreed with his choice, as I had closely followed news of his career. He had beaten American legend Jack Kramer at Wimbledon that summer, before eventually losing in the semi-final, and made the finals of the French Championship at Roland Garros.

I finally obtained permission to transfer to Prague near the end of 1946, where I could study while fulfilling my military obligations. I also continued to consult on the development of our radar systems, with which I was now very familiar. I then contacted my old team, Sparta Prague, and they said my registration was still valid, so I could join them any time I was ready. With that, I moved to Prague in January of 1947, and rejoined Sparta for hockey, while attending university full time. That summer, I completed my two years of military service, and would finish my studies as a civilian. I moved to student housing near Sparta's soccer facilities, which is also where we played hockey. Also nearby was a pub named the Sports Club, owned by Jarda's tennis coach. A group of hockey players would meet there every Friday, and enjoy catching up on each others' lives. What was particularly nice is that it did not matter what team we played for. We were all friends first, and competitors second.

I started the 1947-48 hockey season with Sparta, and I now imagined myself finishing school in Prague, and staying there to pursue a career as an engineer. The bitter memories of the war had begun to fade, and I regained a full measure of optimism for the future. I rediscovered my idealism, and assured myself that we had a tradition of democracy and prosperity, which would surely guide our political destiny. My mood, and that of much of the nation, became openly euphoric when the national hockey team won gold at the World Championships that winter. They were led by Jarda, who scored an amazing fifteen goals in the seven games of the tournament. But I saw little of him after that, as he toured the world playing tennis.

My studies proved much more intense than during my undergraduate days, and by the end of 1947, it became clear that I could not spare the time to also play a full hockey schedule. I then stopped playing for Sparta in January of 1948. This happened just as Czechoslovakia won silver at the Olympics in St. Moritz, once again led by Jarda, who was now considered an international star in two sports. In retrospect, these pleasant distractions allowed much more serious events to creep up on us without adequate scrutiny. That changed in a hurry.

Few people noticed that during the brief time the Soviets occupied our country, they were accompanied by political organizers, who set up local *People's Committees*, and for a time, they represented the country's only organized political structures. This head start enabled them to present a comprehensive slate of candidates for the 1946 elections. They were also aware that a large number of jurisdictions would never elect a communist candidate, so they secretly secured the loyalty of a large number of candidates from other parties. People voted for those candidates, thinking they were in opposition to the Communist Party, but those voters were deceived. The communists did not receive a majority of votes in the 1946 elections, but when their secret allies were added to their total, they controlled a majority of votes in Parliament. Their first act was to form a governing coalition and install Communist Party leader Klement Gottwald as Prime Minister. Once in power, the communists quickly moved to consolidate their control over the police and armed forces, and soon came to dominate all key ministries. The most striking change was in their control over the police, who began to neglect their core functions, and focus mostly on harassing or arresting opponents of the communist coalition. The people were surprised by the abrupt consolidation of power, and early experiences with their heavy handed tactics decisively soured the people on the communists. By 1947, it was widely expected that they would be soundly defeated in elections set for May of 1948, by which time their organizational head start would be nullified. Realizing that this would defeat their ambitions, the communists pressed their advantage while they had it.

On February 12, 1948, the last non-communist members of the National Police Force were terminated, precipitating a political crisis on the 21st, when twelve non-communist Cabinet Ministers resigned under the assumption that this would topple the government. It did not take long for this news to electrify us students in Prague, and we decided that this time, we would not stand by and allow our freedoms to be stolen once again.

I was asked to join a meeting organized by student leaders, near the university. There were perhaps a thousand of us present, on a cold day in late February. The leaders proceeded to paint a dire picture. The communists were systematically replacing the entire bureaucracy with those loyal to themselves. They elaborated on the significance, for anyone who failed to grasp it: Those being installed would ignore the Czechoslovak constitution, and sweep a new, Stalinist order into place. They recounted many examples of the crimes already committed against the people, during and after the war. Now, word was leaking that Prime Minister Gottwald was openly demanding that President Beneš appoint a new cabinet consisting entirely of communists, or those loyal to them. In response to the crisis, we students were asked to organize a demonstration in support of the independence of the

President. I agreed to pass word to fellow students, and prepare for the demonstration.

On the evening of Tuesday, February 24th, 1948, with the communist *coup d'etat* underway, we gathered in front of the headquarters for the Czechoslovak Democratic Party, which was already occupied by the police. We counted about 25,000 students in all, and prepared to march to the President's official residence at Hradčany Castle, on a promontory above the west bank of the Vltava River.

The west bank of the Vltava River. The historic Charles' Bridge is in the foreground. The tall spires at top belong to St. Vitus Cathedral, and the long but irregular building in front of it is Hradčany Castle - the seat of Czech government. The largest part of old Prague is behind this vantage point, on the east side of the river. It was there that the march began.

Inside Hradčany Castle sat President Beneš, probably in the midst of a personal crisis. As much as he justified his decision to capitulate to Hitler's demands in 1938, it must have been made with serious misgivings. Now, ten years later, he was facing a similar demand, only this time from the communists: that he surrender his government, and hand all power over to them. Many factors would have been in play as he contemplated his decision.

There were in excess of a hundred thousand Soviet troops in the eastern province of Ruthenia, ready to move westward at a moment's notice. They stood as a reminder that the communists did not stand alone in their demands. They were implicitly backed by Stalin's military. Beneš had tried to work with the Soviets during the war, but it appeared to buy him no good will in the present standoff. Beneš' staff would certainly have been aware that the Truman administration used the threat of the atomic bomb to force Stalin to back down from his attempts to annex a portion of eastern Turkey, immediately after the war. It is possible that calls were made, hoping to gain the same leverage in Czechoslovakia. But Beneš would have been in the dark about two developments that history has since revealed. First, the Soviets were much closer to their own atomic bomb than anyone in the west imagined they could be, and would not be so easily deterred. Second, the fate of eastern Europe had already been decided. In early 1945, Roosevelt, Churchill, and Stalin met in the Crimean resort town of Yalta, and agreed on a line of control, to avert fighting each other after the fall of Hitler. Beneš would not have known that Czechoslovakia was secretly promised to Stalin, and the allies would have no inclination to risk war over its independence.

Beneš was also well aware that he was not the most popular Czech politician. That honor belonged to Jan Masaryk, son of the late Tomáš Masaryk, who was considered the father of the nation. Masaryk was now the foreign minister, and during his time in London during the second world war, developed close friendships with many top western leaders, not least of whom was King George VI. In addition to being highly charismatic, he came across as much more decisive than Beneš. Beneš would have been aware that people looked to Masaryk as their best hope at that time of crisis. History does not record what opinions were exchanged between the two men, but the presence of a more popular alternative often makes the incumbent feel that much more isolated from the pulse of the people.

The timing of the communists' demands was another important factor. Elections were scheduled in only three months' time, so delay could have been a perfectly reasonable response. Or even a threat to appoint a caretaker cabinet of non-communists until the elections could have had a powerful effect. Both sides would have known this would put an end to the communists' ambitions, which was the very reason they precipitated the crisis at that moment in time. The real problem was Beneš' persistent lack of confidence that the people would unite and back him if it came down to a confrontation, or even violence, over that delay.

That is why the demonstration was organized, and why we students considered it so important. Unlike modern demonstrations that often have little effect, we wanted to demonstrate to both sides that large numbers of us stood for our constitution, and would not sit back and allow our country to be given away a second time. We hoped this would both embolden Beneš to take a stand, and deter Gottwald from escalating the standoff. We were also aware that by its very nature, a demonstration is a challenge to the authority of the government, which could be met with ruthless force. But we were confident that Czech armed forces would take our side, if it came to that.

That evening, word quickly spread that the President was undecided whether to give in to Gottwald's demands. The call went out for an immediate march of everyone we could muster for the following day. Approximately 30,000 of us assembled at three locations in Prague. Once everyone was in place, we began the slow march towards Hradčany. Many older Czechs spontaneously joined us, as did high school students, and our numbers swelled well beyond our wildest ambitions. And it seems the communists were indeed frightened by our numbers. We expected a police presence, and were not intimidated by it. Our numbers were so far in excess of theirs that they could take no meaningful action against us. What we did not expect was the hasty arrival in Prague of heavily armed militia not formally affiliated with the government.

The first group of students reached the historic Charles' Bridge, which crossed the Vltava River below Hradčany. As they began to cross, police and communist militia formed a blockade at the far end, and as the students filled the bridge, another group closed off the bridge from the near end. The students were now bottled up. Police vans appeared at both ends, and began to round up all the students they could, mostly from the ends of the bridge. But their numbers were no match for our demonstration, and gaps soon appeared in their blockade, through which most students escaped. They joined the next group of demonstrators, which crossed the river at a nearby bridge, not attended by the police.

They were led by a flag bearer carrying the Czechoslovak flag, accompanied by others carrying five District Flags. In no time, there were about 30,000 students and many others, marching in the direction of Hradčany. I was close enough to the front that I saw everything that followed. A police unit attempted to halt the flag bearers, but we pushed forward, and overwhelmed the blockade. We continued our march to the seat of government, showing we would not back down when confronted by the militia. We walked slowly through the streets with a serious yet calm demeanor. Nobody was laughing or shouting. I remember seeing classmates, student leaders, other friends from various districts, and even friends from my home town, but we only exchanged perfunctory greetings. Meanwhile, passers-by hailed us, and offered their support, even if they did not join the march. It filled me with pride, knowing that we stood for something good, and the people supported us.

Our leaders and flag bearers reached the first of the narrow streets surrounding Hradčany Castle, where they were met by a very large assembly of militia, armed with rifles and machine guns. They ordered us to disperse, but we refused to move. They were soon joined by dozens of policemen, appearing on all sides of us. Having stood down the police before, our leaders decided to continue marching with the flag bearers, in the face of the assembled militia. At first, the militia began to poke the front rank with their rifle butts, but then someone fired a single shot. After a short pause, during which everyone came to understand the significance of that shot, it was followed by hundreds more. Many students had been hit. I saw two in front of me fall. One was hit by many bullets, and was lying in a pool of blood. Others were bleeding from gunshot wounds, but managed to run away.

We broke ranks once the gunfire erupted, and ran as fast as we could from the vicinity of the Castle. But we were pursued by policemen with machine guns, and the militia armed with Sten sub-machine guns. We scattered in different directions, attempting to evade them. Some students ran into alleys, some up side streets, and some into nearby parks. We ran as fast as we could, pursued by police and militia, shooting with intent to kill. As we passed the people of Prague, their grim faces left a deep impression on me. They were profoundly saddened to see their students being hunted down in the streets. Having lived through the Nazi occupation, they understood the significance of the changes taking place right in front of them.

As President Beneš witnessed the demonstration in support of him getting crushed by overwhelming force, he would have been shocked by the size and armaments of the militia. Indeed, the violence now seems to me to have been intended to do exactly that. Beneš was always unsure of his armed forces, and never appreciated the people's intense desire to live in freedom. Seeing no easy solution, his will gave out, and he signed the order installing an all-communist cabinet. Jan Masaryk was now the lone holdout in government. At first, our hopes fell on him, thinking he was the last one capable of standing down the communists, galvanizing public support, and restoring democracy. But within two weeks, he was found dead in the street, dressed only in his pajamas, in front of his residence at the Foreign Ministry. The official story from the communist-controlled press was that he jumped from his bathroom window, although rumors circulated that it was locked from the inside. The story was widely rejected for many reasons, including that if he chose to commit suicide, knowing the news it would make, he would probably have at least dressed first. The question of whether he was murdered remains unsettled to this day, but it is beyond dispute that his death proved very useful to the new regime, as it marked the end of our hopes that things could be turned around.

Chapter 4: The Crackdown

Demonstrations sprang up all across the country, in opposition to the coup. And in every case, armed militia were positioned in advance, ready to suppress each demonstration with the liberal use of violence. Much smaller counter-demonstrations also took place, where the demonstrators demanded the government formally adopt Marxism. Those demonstrations were protected by the same armed militia, who obviously had an organized command structure, although its nature was not understood at the time.

Every private source of income was immediately nationalized, from large factories to small shops or cafes. Depending on the inclinations of the dispossessed owners, they were allowed to remain as operators of the new state enterprise, or if they protested, they were arrested. All church property was confiscated, and many of the clergy were arrested. If one wonders how the national security forces of the country could be convinced to arrest large numbers of respectable citizens, this was also prepared in advance. The purges executed by the post-war government were designed specifically to replace professionals in the national police force with those considered politically reliable. Then, soon after the coup, people began to disappear. A pattern quickly emerged, where those who went missing included parliamentarians, professors, civil servants, officers of the armed forces, students, and any others who could potentially lead the people against the new regime. Word soon began to spread that lists had been compiled of anyone who could be considered *reactionary* or *unreliable*, and arrests followed. The government had an ever growing supply of political prisoners, most of whom had sentences of twenty five years to life of hard labor. That labor was employed in the uranium mines at Jáchymov, to satisfy Stalin's urgent need of uranium to match the American atom bomb.

The Jáchymov region was once a picturesque valley, bearing the German name *Joachimsthal.* Silver had been discovered in the valley at the beginning of the sixteenth century, leading to the production of a highly prized one-ounce silver coin known as the Joachimsthaler. Across Europe, the name acquired the general meaning of a *fine one-ounce silver coin*, and was soon abbreviated as *Thaler.* It was later adopted into English as *Dollar.* Marie Curie later discovered high levels of radium in the uranite mineral pitchblende, mined from Jáchymov. In the nuclear age, Jáchymov became Europe's prime source of uranium ore. As operations ramped up, it came to light that miners were dying of cancer at very high rates. Radiation exposure also ravaged the immune system, and since political prisoners turned slave laborers had inadequate nutrition and medical care, most in that environment died between the ages of forty and fifty. So those twenty five year sentences were effectively sentences to a slow death.

Many who guessed their names might be on the list of *unreliables* soon began to escape over the borders of Czechoslovakia, mostly to Austria or Germany. As their numbers grew, it became an embarrassment for the regime, which soon decided not to tolerate illegal emigration. The borders were militarized, and anybody trying to cross was shot.

I was making real headway in my studies, and leaving would disrupt everything, so in spite of my involvement in the demonstrations, I did not seriously consider leaving the country. Had I left then, I would everywhere face the problem of getting my patched-together education recognized, and establishing my qualifications in a language I could not speak. Over the course of the spring, I fell into denial about the seriousness of the developing terror. Before the semester was even over, one of my professors had joined the ranks of the missing, as had several students. After we learned this, several of us gathered at a friend's apartment, and discussed the dangers to us.

"All I did was attend the organizational meeting, and subsequent demonstration. How would they even know I was there?" I asked.

"They interrogate those they arrest," was one answer. "For all we know, they're collecting names."

I came away concerned, but not enough to want to emigrate. I knew many fellow students who were at the demonstration, and most of them were still free. I could see that a malignant change was underway, but I told myself we had been through worse with the Nazis. In truth, it was simply easier to imagine finishing my education, and if things continued to worsen, then consider leaving after that.

As all of this was going through my head, I was still living in student residence, near the Sparta sports facility. One day there was an unexpected knock on my door, and for the first time, I began to fear that one day, a knock like this could be the police, coming to arrest me. I opened the door with some apprehension, but I brightened up immediately when I saw the visitor. It was Jarda Drobný, who I had not seen in some time. "It's great to see you". I began to tell him how I had followed the national hockey team at the St. Moritz Olympics, but he interrupted me.

"Do you have a few moments to talk, somewhere private?"

We walked the short distance to his residence at the tennis club where I had once also played hockey. It was on an island in the middle of the river, so it was as private a spot as anyone could find in the city. It was obvious that this was not a simple social call, but I continued to hope it had something to do with hockey. Once we were on the island, he began.

"I went on a tennis tour, after the Olympics."

"I know all about it. The papers were getting ready to denounce you as a traitor for defecting, but then you came back. They said you came down with some sickness, and stayed out of sight for a while."

"Carl, the papers were closer to the truth than you know."

"You considered defecting?" I asked, incredulously. Jarda was a national hero, and would have lost his status entirely.

"The only reason I didn't leave was because England would not grant me residency. I only made up the story to cover my tracks."

I stared at him, still unable to believe my ears. "You once said you'd never leave."

He nodded, but continued. "I meet a lot of people, so I hear a lot of things. And it's getting bad. They don't trust me in the slightest, and one day when I'm no longer winning, I expect they'll arrest me. I trust you'll never tell anyone I told you this, but I have one more important thing to tell you."

"Go ahead," I said, apprehensively.

"When I returned, I was subjected to a long

interrogation. They spent a lot of time asking about my hockey contacts. It seems they have their eye on hockey players, for whatever reason. I mostly told them we did not discuss politics; girls and sports were far more interesting. But then they asked if I was still in touch with you."

"They mentioned me by name?"

"Yes. They know you were associated with the organizers of the demonstration. Carl, I think you seriously need to consider getting out. I might not be far behind."

Even with that warning from a friend who was also a hero to me, I could not bring myself to leave the country. But I took some precautions. As the semester ended, I moved out of the student residence and into a private apartment, but I did not change the address on any paperwork that could be traced back to me. I had started a summer job, and even on their paperwork, I listed my address as the student residence. I hoped this could buy me some time. I would hear that they came to look for me at the student residence, and use that as my cue to leave town. My plan was to return home to Moravia, where I knew the countryside better than any communist thug, and I could hide for some time. I also knew all the good places to cross the border into Austria, if it came down to that.

As that summer passed, and more students, professors, and others disappeared, my friends would often bring up the topic of leaving the country. But none of us were willing to be the first of our circle of friends to do so. If Jarda had defected, and been denounced in the news, I might have had a cathartic moment. I knew there was not a traitorous bone in his body, and I might have followed him out. Every time someone disappeared, we had the same discussions, and agreed it might be prudent to get ready to leave. But then we returned to our routines, and life felt normal again, so we did nothing.

Another semester started at school, and I started to think maybe they were not interested in me after all. Jarda warned me in April or May. It was now September, and nothing had happened. I remained complacent until that day when it happened. And of course, by then it was too late.

Chapter 5: Bottoming Out

Lying in that dark cell and unable to stop the bleeding from my ordeal, I resigned myself to the certainty that I was going to die. I had been hit on the head many times, and was dizzy, even nauseous. It would probably come soon, and the pain would at least be over. I thought of my brother, and whether he suffered like this before they killed him. But I did not feel sorry for myself, or much of anything else. It was simply the cold realization that this was how it would end. If I was lucky. Otherwise, I would die slowly in the uranium mines, over twenty years or so. Either way, I clung to no hope of escaping my fate. So many others had gone before me. Why should I be any different? I was also being realistic. Nobody was going to break into this prison complex, risking their lives to rescue me. And even if someone did, how far could we get?

One of my cell mates died that first night. Probably from head wounds stemming from his interrogation. I never learned his name. As they removed his body the following morning, I could not help but envy him. Unlike the rest of us, he was now beyond their reach. I might have stayed in that cell another day, or at least part of a day. Without natural light, it was impossible to track the passage of time, and my head injuries made me unable to focus on anything very well. But I remember when the order came to move out. It was dark outside. They herded us into army trucks, and I assumed we were heading for the uranium mines. But what I expected to be a long ride to Jáchymov turned into a short ride to

Stochov, west of the city of Kladno, not far from Prague. It was the location of a large network of concentration camps, set up to temporarily hold the countless political prisoners the communists were arresting. For the first time since my arrest, I remembered looking around at those arriving with me, some 200 by my estimate, and seeing the battered, bruised and swollen faces and bodies, in some cases still seeping blood or fluid. We were herded into a large field bordered by barbed wire, and told to slowly walk in large circles, around the field. We did this for an hour or so, and one man who could not keep up with the pace was taken away by the guards. I wondered whether the purpose of this exercise was to identify those too weak to be of any use as laborers. And if so, did that mean those prisoners would be executed? I had my suspicions, but no evidence.

We were then assigned housing in a temporary structure that was a cross between a barn and a large tent. "I was afraid we'd be in Jáchymov by now," I said to several others, clustered together.

"They have far more slave laborers than they can accommodate just yet," came a reply from another battered man. He looked to be in his late thirties, and we chatted for a while. He had been a parliamentarian opposed to the communists, and now he too was given a life sentence in the uranium mines. But through his contacts, he had learned that while the Soviet Union placed a high premium on Czech uranium ore, they had run into logistical snags ramping up their mining operations, which is why we were here, waiting. I remember expressing surprise that he could be arrested for expressing opinions in Parliament, but he pointed to a number of other prisoners in similar circumstances. There were military personnel, civil servants, politicians and professors. All we had in common was that the new regime saw us as a potential threat.

Besides that one brief conversation, nobody was willing to speak, or interact in any way during those first days. I thought constantly of my brother.

Dear brother when I last saw you,
Your eyes betrayed a depth of sorrow,
Weighed down with regrets over our fate,
Your soul seemed burdened with foreknowledge.

We had always been close,
In those joyful moments of our youth,
Your inner beauty lit my path,
A sweet contrast to this cruel truth.

I've cherished the memories of those beautiful days,
How gladly you worked for our food,
Every moment with you was like a dream,
You unfailingly led me to everything good.

I still see you, my big brother, tussling your hair,
The sun shining on your face,
Your touch embraces me as gently as a flower,
As we walk to tend the vines.

I admired your strong arms,
I cherished the sound of your voice,
I clung to your words in the silence of the forest,
Surrounded by the fragrance of moss.

I still see you waving at me in the vineyard,
To assure me I was not alone,
I still smell the roses you gave me,
I cherish the songs you taught me.

The day came when they took you from us,
And put you in their murderous cells,

Bottoming Out

It became a source of morbid curiosity that new people came in unrecognizable, with their swollen eyes and battered faces. Then over the next week or so, here and there, I would recognize someone as their faces returned to normal. The spirits of most new prisoners were as broken as my own, and they obeyed every command from the guards. But there were exceptions. One man, ordered to get into line at one of the roll calls, barked back at the guard, something to the effect that he had no business ordering him around. The guard casually impaled him with his bayonet, and laughed coldly as his body slumped to the ground, in view of all of the rest of us. I was too numb to feel much of anything at that moment, but over the course of the next several days, I seriously considered making a run for it. The field was ringed with barbed wire, which would slow me down enough to ensure I would be shot, but that was the whole point. To end it on my terms, and not theirs. As the days passed, and I realized I did not have the gumption to do it, I felt even more defeated than when they first arrested me. I was still certainly going to die, but it would be slowly, in the uranium mines.

At first, the swelling on my own face covered up my emotions, but as that subsided, I became aware that I was sobbing for long stretches of time. And so were most of those whose faces also had time to heal.

The guards seemed to know our disposition, too. Anyone who was off by himself for some quiet time, a time for tears, was a target for harassment. "You want to cry, like a baby? I'll give you a reason to cry like a baby," was a favorite line. It was usually accompanied by a beating from a rifle butt, or Billy-club.

It had been more than a week since I arrived, when my face healed enough that I again looked like myself, that I was first recognized by an old friend from the University. I did not recognize him at first, because he was newer, but hearing his voice raised my spirits right away. We walked together during our daily walk around the field, and began to chat a little too much for the sensibilities of the guards. A rifle butt to the ribs, and a rude remark, was a reminder that we had to speak discreetly. I also think another guard with a notepad recorded our names, for what that was worth. If we were all considered traitors, was it not logical that some of us would be friends?

In the following days, I began to recognize other students, professors, and even people I knew from childhood, in my home town. It was then that the scale of the arrests finally sunk in. I was never an organized revolutionary, and before seeing them all in the camp, had no idea any of these people had any political inclinations at all. The only things we had in common were opposition to communism, and public prominence, or the potential for it, in the case of university students. What was in progress was a great purge of all of Czechoslovak society, to ensure that communist voices were the only ones heard in the public square.

In spite of our imprisonment and pending fate, I felt some joy at recognizing so many friends, and my attitude matured, although not for the last time. If it was going to be a short life in the uranium mines, at least I'd be surrounded by people of integrity. I convinced myself I would rather serve my sentence and die early with these good people, than live in luxury surrounded by the kinds of depraved people responsible for our suffering. I never had that choice, so I can't be sure I would have chosen a slow death over being communist. But it gave me some strength to believe it. It was always a struggle to keep up my spirits, so I think I coaxed myself into believing what I needed to believe, to get through another day.

One day a few weeks later, as I was walking in the field, a new prisoner, still bearing his introductory wounds, made a point of bumping into me, and whispered, "I thought I'd find you here."

I had no idea who he was. It was only after he spoke for a few seconds more, and said my name, that I recognized it was Jan, my old family friend. I turned to face him and wanted to hug him, sympathetic to how he must be feeling right now, but he abruptly turned away from me. At first I was taken aback, but then he whispered, "I have a plan. Pretend you don't know me, for now."

I did as he said, but from then on, I always kept one eye on him, to observe his interactions with other prisoners. And I quickly noticed that Jan was systematically making contact with many of my friends and acquaintances. It was only then that I convinced myself that Jan might have privileged information, and a plan with a chance of success. He had risen through the military, and before the coup was the commander of all armed forces in the southwest region of the country. He was purged sometime during the summer, and presumably arrested after I was. But it would realistically take the communists several years to replace all junior officers with experienced communist replacements, so he probably had an ideal list of contacts.

He assembled a group consisting of two of our professors, Jiri and Antonin, fellow students Frank, Peter, Josef, Dusan, Viktor, Zdenek, and myself, all from Charles University. Then there was Pavel, Cenek, Michal, Bohumil, and Evžen from universities in Brno or Bratislava. Rudolf and Hynek were formerly with the police, but having joined us at the student demonstrations, were purged by the communists. I had already met Robert the former parliamentarian, and Jan found one other, named Jurek. Also in Jan's circle was another former military man, Borek, who had been a senior security officer. Borek also seemed to know everyone in the camp, especially those in our group.

We knew to be careful when we met, and spoke. The housing facility was constantly monitored, and we dared not risk walking over to one of our party and starting a discussion. But during our hour-long walks through the field every day, there was a constant shuffling of people, and most exchanged a few words with everyone as they passed each other. It was during this time that we learned to inconspicuously pass word among ourselves, careful to make the interaction quick, and the words, few. Jan let the group know that he had developed his plan as a contingency, some time ago, and expected help from within the system.

I could not ask openly, so I had to fill in the details for myself. Jan formed our group from people he knew, or who knew each other well. I also observed that we were all young, or if a little older, in good physical shape. Regrettably, whatever he had in mind could not help those who were too old, or too weak, to take part in his plan.

As I imagined the fanciful details that Jan might have cooked up, I felt a sense of hope return to me. Not because I was confident the plan would succeed. My eyes were open to our long odds. Any one of the key contacts Jan had assembled could be arrested at any time, leaving us without the lifelines we were going to count on. But we would attempt to escape, and that meant things would happen on our initiative. If we failed, we would die trying. But that would still be a victory of sorts, because it would be death on our terms. It would not be the slow death in the uranium mines that the communists had in store for us. And that was enough to keep me committed to the plan.

Several months passed, and winter set it. December turned to January, and we received word that we would soon be leaving for the uranium mines. The weather was damp and misty, which I knew would be far better for our chances than if there were deep snow. When the day came, there was an announcement that all prisoners would soon be departing, and every man was assigned to one of three groups. The first two groups were composed of about 300 men each, while we fell into a third group with roughly 160 prisoners. The first two groups were quickly herded into empty railroad box cars, waiting nearby. We stood a short distance away, watching the prisoners enter the box cars. We began to whisper among ourselves that escape would be impossible if we were loaded in those box cars, with their strong doors that latched from the outside. Nervously, we looked to Jan and Borek, who nodded, and motioned for us to be patient. Once loading was complete, the train departed, and some 600 of our compatriots departed for the harsh conditions and toxic contamination of the uranium mines.

With the train having departed, we were ordered back to our housing, where we spent one more night. I did my best not to look like I was paying attention to Jan or Borek, but of course, I was. I was as nervous as I've ever been that night, and barely slept a wink. In the middle of the night, I heard some commotion, and stole a peek in Jan's direction. I saw an unfamiliar uniformed man deliver a small package to him, before leaving quietly.

Chapter 6: Escape

They assembled us outdoors again the following day, and large trucks covered with an ordinary military grade canopy arrived to collect our group. But then everything came to a stop. Nothing happened over the course of the whole day, so we stood around, stewing with anxiety. It was not until evening that the order came to load the remainder of the prisoners into the trucks. Jan passed word to our group to be ready for the last truck. Jan's entire circle managed to be in the group loaded into the final truck, holding thirty men. Twenty were members of our circle, but there were ten additional men we did not know. Following Jan's lead, we positioned ourselves to be at the back of the truck, allowing the ten strangers to sit near the front, where it was less drafty, and the ride was more comfortable. We had only our prison jackets, and a small bag containing our documents, to be presented to officials in Jáchymov. But everyone suspected that Jan and Borek had more items hidden away.

We were ordered to remain standing in the truck, until two guards came through and counted everyone. We were then ordered to sit. One guard left, and soon came back with ropes. A third soon joined them, and together, they secured a rope to the side of the truck, and tied two tight loops of rope on each prisoner's right hand, so we were all tied together. Once they had finished, the guards started with a second rope, securing it to the side of the truck, and looping it twice around the chest of each prisoner, leaving us little room to move. Two of the guards then left for the front of the convoy, while a third, assigned to guard us, joined the driver in the front of the truck.

Then we waited. The trucks were idling, but we were sitting still. I kept worrying that they were going to change logistics at the last minute, and spoil Jan's plan. But the convoy departed as soon as it was dark. The roads were very twisty, and the trucks often had to slow down for curves. It was also quite bumpy, jostling us around in the back. About an hour into the trip, most of the men were fast asleep, in spite of the constant jostling. I was drifting in and out myself, but at one point, I saw Jan give a nod to Borek. As if on cue, they both bent the fabric of a section of their clothing with some force, causing the knives that had been sewn in to cut through the fabric. They passed the knives along, and our two police security men quietly cut the long ropes wrapped around our chests. As quickly as we were able, we silently wiggled out of those ropes, helping each other along the way. The ten men not in our group were sleeping soundly, and the guard in the front of the truck seemed tired. I never saw him look through his window into the back of the truck.

With us clustered around the back of the truck, Jan and Borek turned their attention to the canopy across the back. They began to work it with their knives, and it seemed to be taking far longer than it should. Their manner betrayed their tension, which was infectious. If they could not manage to cut through that canopy in time, the whole plan would be in jeopardy. My heart was pounding furiously, knowing that at any moment, the ten men not with us could awake, and in their surprise cause enough commotion to alert the guards. Finally, after extensive effort, they cut through the truck's canopy.

We then waited for the truck to slow down for a sharp bend in the road, and Jan gave the signal. As many of us were still tied to each other by the rope on our right wrist, we slid through the gap in the canopy in rapid succession, and out of the truck. We hit the ground gently, and the last man jumped just as the truck was starting to pick up speed as it exited the curve.

We quickly hid ourselves in dense hedges at the edge of the road, where Jan and Borek took count of us. They instructed us to remove the remaining ropes from our right hands, which we did gladly. We then gathered the scraps of rope, and hid them in the hedge, to avoid alerting anyone of where we made our escape. "Let's put some distance between them and us," said Jan.

Breathing heavily, we ran at the fastest pace we could sustain, in two rows, through dense undergrowth. Thick branches scratched us everywhere, and a few received puncture wounds from branches, but we did not let that slow us. We had all endured much worse at the hands of the communists, and under no circumstances would we risk falling back into their hands.

We maintained an intense pace all night, walking briskly and often running, always avoiding roads and villages. We rested in forests, and other undeveloped areas, but never for very long. As the sun came up, we came to a clearing where we could be seen from nearby roads. We crossed the clearing in an all out sprint, and were utterly exhausted. A short time later, we came to a deep forest with large trees, and found a relatively deep ditch. We took cover in the ditch, and rested for several hours. Rudolf, who had been a policeman, knew this part of the country very well from his previous work. He had even crossed the border with various people, before it had been militarized. So he went ahead alone, to try to determine where we were.

Anticipating his return was as nerve-wracking as any experience that day. What if he were caught? Would he lead them to us, to save himself? He returned about a half hour after he left, with the news that we had escaped from the truck convoy near the town of Lubenec. In the time we had been on the move, we had passed the small town Nečtiny, and were close to the village of Dolní Bělá. Imagining those places on a map in my head, I estimated we had covered some forty kilometers since our escape. Exhausted as we were, this news raised our spirits considerably, as we knew we were headed in the right direction. I knew we had to go south, and cross the border to the American Zone of Germany somewhere in the Šumava Forest, contiguous with the German Black Forest. Given that the truck was bound for Jáchymov, Lubenec was the perfect place for us to make our escape. Jan had planned very well, after all.

While resting, we took the opportunity to remove our prison vests, and hid them deep in the bushes. "We need to reach an intersection where my contacts should be waiting for us," said Jan. *How did he plan this down to the smallest detail?,* I wondered, briefly. I reminded myself that during my stint in the military, I was mostly tied up with questions of radar, but as a commander, Jan was a professional planner.

We ran for a short interval, minimizing the time we spent in view of houses and streets, then walked for an hour or two more. Then as the short Czech winter day began to wane, we came to Jan's intersection. He signaled to us to keep quiet, while he confirmed his contacts had arrived. We could see a blinking light in the distance, which he took that as his signal, and led us to two small trucks, and an ordinary car. One of the drivers quickly approached Jan and Borek, and after a few words, Jan called to us. They ordered us into the trucks, while our leaders got into the car, which took the lead. In the darkness, we could not make out any landmarks, so we could not tell which way we were being driven. The drive was long, and the lack of information was very unnerving. It was one thing to trust Jan implicitly while there was no choice, back in the prison. But now that running off alone was an option, it took more faith in Jan, in the absence of information.

That faith was put to the test when we rounded a curve and had to stop abruptly, because the police had set up a checkpoint. They spoke with those in the front car, but in the back truck, I had no idea what was happening. The driver yelled at us to remain silent, and out of sight. We arranged a loose tarp in the back to cover all of us. Eventually, they walked around to our truck, and I could hear voices I did not recognize. Jan's was not among them.

"What sort of weapons are you carrying?" asked the policeman.

"It's not my place to ask. The cases are sealed, and it's prison for anyone opening them without authorization. You want to risk that?"

The policeman said nothing, but walked around the truck, seemingly afraid to even look inside. "We're looking for a group of escaped prisoners. Have you seen a bunch of about twenty, all dressed alike?"

The driver was silent too long for my comfort. Finally, he replied, "A few people here and there, but not twenty. And everyone seems dressed alike, anyhow. Are they dangerous?"

The policeman did not answer. He continued to walk around the trucks, while we tried not to even breathe.

"Which border checkpoint are you delivering your weapons to?"

"Železná Ruda."

There was silence. I was praying he would not know we were a little too far east to be credibly heading there. His accent was Moravian, so with any luck, he would not know the area too well. I could hear the footsteps receding, and more discussion in the distance. It felt like we had been there half an hour, but as suddenly as we had stopped, we began moving again.

I managed to relax a little after that, and dozed off briefly. I was awakened when the truck stopped, and the drivers ordered us out.

"What's going on, now?" asked one of the others.

"Sušice ahead," answered the driver. "The place is going to be swarming with checkpoints and patrols. We barely bluffed the last one, and that's only because he was stupid. No way will the pros believe my line a second time."

We got out in a hurry, and the drivers quickly turned around and left the area. We were now alone, and Jan looked nervous. "Sušice is where the whole border security apparatus is headquartered. We'll have to stay away from all the roads, now. Especially since they're looking for us."

By my estimate, the trucks had driven us a distance of about a hundred kilometers. It would have been nearly impossible to complete this trip without that ride, and it made me appreciate Jan's contacts that much more. He led us through the darkness, sometimes running, and I was amazed how he seemed to know every forest path along the way. Either he had rehearsed this route before, or he was an excellent navigator, without the benefit of starlight to orient himself. We rested occasionally but were always on edge, and ready to flee at a moment's notice. We came to a bridge over a small river, and Jan announced that we would wait there for our next contact. We took cover in a ditch behind some dense trees, and soon heard sounds and voices. Someone was walking in our direction. The tension grew, and we prepared ourselves to break into a run. Jan moved towards the voices, while we remained hidden. He returned in no time, accompanied by a forest ranger, carrying two hunting rifles. Jan introduced him as Foltýn. The Ranger explained where we were, and led us through dense forest, until we came to an old cottage he owned, surrounded by trees. He inspected it quickly, then invited us inside. Inside, he put his bag on the dusty floor, while keeping one of his rifles on his arm. "Nobody knows about this place," he assured us.

Foltýn met with our leaders, and left them instructions for our next steps. He then opened the bag he had earlier dropped on the floor, and to our surprise, handed out sandwiches and fruit. He then shook hands with each of us, wished us luck, and left, taking his rifles with him. Until that moment, we had not even thought about food, but now realized we were very hungry. We finished our meal quickly, and rested as long as we could. Meanwhile, Jan left us again. Nervously, we waited for his return, and our next move. He came back with four friends of his, and introduced them as the ones he had been waiting for. They all carried guns, and had served in the military under Jan. All four were also bound for the west, ostensibly for England. But in the meantime, they gave Jan guns and a lot of ammunition, which he distributed to his military and police friends within our group.

Jan and Borek were also given a detailed map, showing exactly where we could find hiding places, and what locations we should avoid. They could not stress enough how important it was to choose the right place to cross the border, and they made recommendations, but they also warned that additional communist militia were constantly being added to the border zones, so the situation was subject to change at any time. They wished us luck, and then departed for their own journey to the west. At least we knew that the borders were not uniformly well patrolled, and there were still gaps that made it possible to escape. We were also assured that the local people in the villages would help us if they could, without endangering themselves. It occurred to me that Jan could have left with the four of them, leaving us to fend for ourselves. It was a testament to his sense of responsibility that he chose to stay with us.

A light rain soon began to fall. We stayed in the small cottage until the first light of day, and slept lightly for only a couple of hours. We were acutely aware that our disappearance had been noticed, and alarms had gone out. Those would only intensify once they realized Jan was among us, given the value of his military knowledge. Then we began to worry whether they could track us, and anticipate which way we were going. As we stopped to ponder all the possibilities, our initial optimism at escaping began to fade. We were facing long odds, which did not seem to matter while we were in prison and expecting to go to Jáchymov, but now that we were close, the odds began to matter. And what would await us at the border? We knew security at the borders was highly fluid, and we could not anticipate how many communist guards and soldiers would be in place when and where we attempted our crossing. And we were far from the only ones trying to cross the border and escape. People from all walks of life were attempting it, most without a good plan. They were often doomed to being shot, and if we were anywhere in their vicinity, we would be caught in the lines of fire. With these concerns on our minds, we set out, with Jan paying careful attention to the route we were taking. We pushed through dense trees, and up a steep hill, made slippery by the falling rain.

We stopped a little while after noon, when we came to a patch of flat ground, and quietly huddled to review our plan. In the distance was a main road, and it seemed from our relatively safe distance that about half the vehicles passing by were some form of police or military. The communists had deported most of the residents of the surrounding villages, and militarized the entire region, as it was favored by those trying to escape to Germany. Anyone we met at this point was odds-on a communist militia member. We continued, and later in the afternoon, Rudolf quietly announced that we were approaching the town of Modrava. Many of us knew the name, and this meant we were now in the Šumava Forest, leading to the Border Zone. Then Jan asked with some concern, "Rudko, how do you know this?"

"The brook we just crossed. It runs into the Vydra just over that way."

"We're too close," objected Jan. He was

interrupted by the rumbling of a heavy truck approaching.

"Into the forest. Now," he said, firmly but quietly.

We ran with what energy we had left, towards the nearby tree line. No sooner were we in the forest than we heard the shout: "Stop right there."

We did not even slow down, and the man noticed. He pulled his pistol and took two shots in our direction. I initially thought it was three shots, but I was near the front of the group, so I did not see that Hynek shot back, and found his target. Jan gave up the pretense of whispering, and shouted, "run."

We had been seen, and it would be only a short time before the dead official was reported missing. Once they found him, they would know to be on the lookout for us. They could make a good guess where we were headed, and it would not be a stretch for them to deduce that we were the group they were looking for. Running and walking, as the terrain and our energy levels allowed, we made our way as far into the Šumava forest as was within our strength. Finally after dark, we came to the edge of a small ridge, then entered a very thick forest, covering a hill in front of us. Ahead was an old cottage, so Jan had us hide in the thick of the forest and went alone, to get a closer look at the cottage. He then waved us over, indicating it was clear to enter. "Foltýn told me about this one."

Chapter 7: Through the Valley of Death

Having traversed another thirty kilometers on foot since the trucks dropped us off, we were in desperate need of some rest, so we set up shifts for each man to stand guard, while the rest of us lied down and huddled together for what turned out to be a night of light sleep, as I kept imagining freedom, and rehearsing our final escape in my head. Soft rain resumed towards morning, but it now mixed with snowflakes. When the final guard woke everyone, nobody felt like they needed more sleep, and nobody was under any illusions over our fate if we failed to escape. If they caught so much as a glimpse of us, blood would be spilled. Jan decided the chances were too high that we might all be caught or killed if we crossed as one group. So he split us up into three separate groups, to spread the risk. The left side group consisted of Jan, Rudolf, Jiri, Robert, Pavel and Zdenek. In the center group were Frank, Dusan, Bohumil, Cenek, Michal, Evžen, and myself. On the right side were Borek, Antonin, Hynek, Jurek, Peter, Josef, and Viktor. There were two armed men with each of the outer groups, but none in my center group. We spread apart about fifteen meters, under the rationale that if one group was targeted, it would incur heavy casualties, but perhaps the others could escape undetected. The ground was a little harder than the soggy earth we had earlier traversed, and a light wind came up at us from the west. Snow was falling gently on the surrounding mountains in front of us. Looking across the valley to our left, we saw what we guessed was Mount Rachel, in the German

Black Forest. To our right was Mount Falkenstein. We were close enough to see freedom, but that only meant we were in the thick of the highly patrolled Border Zone.

The valley we crossed, photographed in spring, slightly west of our crossing point, where the old barbed wire is on the Czech side of the valley. The view looks towards Germany. Photographed many years later, with forests having been thinned out.

"God be with us. We'll all meet up on the other side," said Jan. With that, we began the descent into the valley, nestled between mountains. The ground was very hard, and densely covered by small pines. When we saw the hastily assembled and disjointed barbed wire fortifications, I felt like we could actually succeed. We moved forward, with my center group taking the lead by about ten meters, watching our surroundings constantly. We hid in the dense trees whenever we could, moving forward slowly and deliberately. In spite of having slept little, and eaten nothing for about thirty six hours, I had no trouble mustering the energy to carry on. But I feared some of the others might be running out of energy after so much walking and running. Still fearful, we looked around for any movement. At first we experienced quiet, with only the sounds of our own footsteps, and the peaceful sounds of the forest. But all of a sudden, multiple heavy vehicles burst out of the depths of the forest less than a hundred meters from us, giving us almost no time to drop to the ground, and cover ourselves with a few branches. Sound did not carry well where we had chosen to cross, so we would not hear them until they were almost right upon us. Peering through the trees and lower bushes, we saw two police vehicles, manned by communist guards, followed closely by one military vehicle. Each vehicle carried a mounted machine gun.

We stayed hidden until the police and military vehicles had passed, then carefully surveyed the area, particularly the upper section of the wide valley with steep sides. The border was part of the way up the far side of the valley, so to reach safety, we would have to make it most of the way to the top of the other side before they saw us. "We need to lay low for a while, to learn how often they pass," said Cenek. I could not hear what Jan was telling his group, but I was sure Cenek had it right.

Staying hidden, we timed how long it took for the vehicles to make a few more passes. What we saw complicated matters. The military truck took longer to make its rounds, while the police vehicles made more regular passes, so it was never going to be a regular interval. We could wait until the military vehicle passed together with the police vehicles, giving us a window of maybe ten minutes until the next pass of the police vehicles. But that was not going to be enough time for us to make it to the top of the far side of the valley. It was further complicated because many fresh trails had been cut through the forest, allowing the patrols to drive their vehicles right up to the border, where previously there was only dense forest. And we did not know where all the fresh trails were. We had been warned that the communists were militarizing the border, but seeing the scale of it still came as shock.

It was not difficult to muster the nerve to move forward. I think we all knew this was going to be our last, best chance to escape. We continued to hold our position for nearly an hour, hiding in the dense undergrowth on the sloping valley wall, and carefully observed the patrols. As I had surmised, Jan was waiting for the military vehicle to pass together with the police vehicles. As soon as it did, Jan whistled, giving us the signal, and his left group began to move forward. Having previously agreed on our plan, Michal and I took the lead, to scout out the fortifications ahead. Moving on our hands and knees, we took every opportunity to peer through the undergrowth. Half way down the hill, we encountered sections of barbed wire with gaps between them, and where they were contiguous, the posts were weakly planted in the ground, and the wires were low to the ground. I briefly smiled at this blessing of communist inefficiency. The Nazis would have had everything buttoned down.

Michal and I hastily returned to our group, and filled them in on what we saw, again taking cover in ditches or other low spots, in dense foliage. Then out of nowhere, police vehicles exploded from the forest, very close to us this time. It was disheartening how we would have no advance warning of their approach.

Seeing that they were clear, we exchanged signals, confirming that it was time for the whole group to move. We moved into the valley and closed in on the barbed wires. The others all breathed a sigh of relief when they saw they were low to the ground, and loose, so we could bend them with ease. They were still sharp, but they were passable. And they were not electrified, another factor we had feared. But we were running out of time, and were still far from safety.

The police vehicles burst out of the forest on schedule, and we were vulnerable. I hoped everyone would be able to get under tree branches in time, but several of our group had been lagging. I suspected something was amiss when the police vehicles stopped nearby. They stopped close enough to us that we heard a lot of shouting, although we could not make out any words. Then the military vehicle roared into view, and also stopped. *Why would they have stopped, unless we had been spotted?* I ducked down into low foliage where I was, knowing it was better not to be seen than to try to outrun the patrols. My fears were realized when the machine guns opened fire. Perhaps someone panicked, and ran, although I never learned exactly what tipped them off. There was now no choice, so we all got up and ran. I could not see where the shots were coming from, and maybe I was lucky that the contour of the land kept me out of their line of fire. Ahead, the last line of barbed wires was tantalizingly close. I kept running, until something violently threw me forward and to the ground. I found myself in a lot of pain, in many places. There was an intense burning in my side, and my hand, and ankle, were in severe pain. Looking around, I saw my colleagues were all bleeding. I looked at my own body, and I was bleeding as badly as they were. We now crawled on our knees, desperate to reach the last row of barbed wire. The right group was behind us and briefly turned to their right. That was met by another flare-up of gunfire, but now we also heard dogs barking, only a short distance behind us. When we got to the barbed wire fence, two of us bent the loops of wire, flattening them so the others could slide over.

After clearing the fence, Frank, Cenek and I bent the wire loops even further, to help those coming up behind us. Bohumil, Michal, and Evžen were right behind us, and we helped them pull themselves over the wires. We were all bleeding from multiple wounds, and bullets continued to spray the area. Then we saw Dusan, slowly crawling towards us and bleeding heavily from what seemed to be serious wounds. Despite our own wounds, Frank and I quickly decided to go back and help him. Our colleagues pushed us over the wires, and we crawled on our knees back in his direction. We grabbed his arms and carried him in the direction of wire fence. "Save yourselves," objected Dusan, but we dismissed his words. With Evžen's help, we lifted Dusan over the bent fence and took him to dense undergrowth where we were hidden, part of the way up the far side of the valley.

Behind us, the left group had been hit hard by gunfire, and were also being chased by dogs. Instead of making for our position, they turned to the left a little. That exposed them to direct gunfire, so they quickly turned back in our direction. Peering through the branches, we saw Borek, Antonin, Jurek and Peter slowly crawling on their knees towards the fences. The gunfire was not abating, and the dogs were approaching, but several of us crossed back a second time, moving as quickly as we were able, given our wounds, and helped them pull themselves across the fence. Peter was badly wounded, so we carried him to higher ground. Frank, Evžen and I were last to reach the dense thicket, and we thought most of us had made it across. But a quick glance told us otherwise.

We saw Hynek fall to the ground in a fight with the communist militia guards. They hit him with their rifle butts, but he still had his revolver. As he fell, he managed to shoot two of the militia. But it was too late. More policemen arrived as backup, and filled him with bullets at short range, including a short burst of Sten gun fire. Bullets were still hitting the forest in our vicinity, but we looked back again and saw dogs attacking Josef and Viktor. The dogs latched on to their arms, legs and throats. There was so much blood, they must have severed major arteries. We watched, with tears in our eyes, as the militia finished them off with bursts of gunfire, at close range. From our hiding place in a small ditch behind dense bush, we moved on. Our pace was now a crawl, with our wounds making any movement extremely painful. If they decided to follow us, there was nothing more we could have done to escape. Exhausted, badly wounded and bleeding, we could not continue any farther. We cleaned the blood from our eyes, and looked around to see who was still with us.

The higher ground at top of the valley was so close, but we could not continue any further. We all collapsed where we were, resigned to our fates. The gunfire had stopped, but that could simply mean they were closing in on us, and did not want to shoot each other. When we heard loud voices nearby, we were sure it was the militia closing in on us. A few of us struggled to get up, but we had nothing left. They would find us, and finish us off, after all. And a few seconds later, we were surrounded by soldiers, with guns.

Then the soldiers' leader spoke to us in broken Czech, "You are now in the International Zone, American section. You're safe here. We saw everything, and we admire your courage." Another soldier spoke to us, again in broken Czech, "It was sad to see your three colleagues die horribly, like they did." Most or all of us broke down and cried at that point. Several of us made a sign of the cross, and with one voice, said loudly, "May God bless them and receive them."

The American soldiers first took Dusan, then Jurek and Peter, with the worst wounds. They carried them to their vehicles, and drove them to the U.S. Army Field Hospital. The other soldiers then took the rest of us to different U.S. Army Medical Facilities. We received medical attention for many wounds caused by bullets, shrapnel from hand grenades, broken bones, and deep gashes caused by branches and barbed wire. Michal had a broken left hand and a bullet in his back. Evžen had a broken right hand, wrist, and multiple leg wounds. Frank and I both had small pieces of shrapnel removed from our abdomens, hands and shoulders. We both had broken fingers, and I had a broken ankle. Jurek and Peter had chest wounds, and were hospitalized for some time. All we knew about Dusan is that he required surgery two days in a row.

Our approximate border crossing location is marked with an X.
To the east is Modrava, and Sušice is at the top of the map. Even
today, the area is mostly undeveloped wilderness.

Chapter 8: We're Glad You're Safe, ... But ...

It was closing in on a year since the demonstration, and four months since my arrest. I had survived, although I can't say the same for Hynek, Josef and Viktor. My injuries would heal, I was assured, and the other survivors would likewise live normal lives. But what was normal? If asked a year ago, normal would be finishing up my doctorate, and working on my country's radar systems. Now, I was facing the prospect of a life in exile in whatever country would take me, a new language, and a complete disconnect from the remnants my family and closest friends. I may have been financially poor, but I once had what I regarded as a rich life, and now I had lost every last piece of that treasure. On the other hand, I was extremely grateful for my second chance at living a life. Whatever it held in store, it would be an honest life, lived on my terms. It was a huge relief that the nightmare was behind me, although it took many years for me to get over it in my heart. For the time being, I was surrounded by others in the same circumstances, so I found comfort in fellowship. And I had important short-term objectives: I had to heal physically, and find a new home. I would not worry about what came after that.

After seven days of recuperation, we were called to meet with the commanding officer. He had helped us with everything we needed, but now he could not resist weighing in as a strategist. "Had you turned more towards Mount Rachel, your escape would have been easier. We've got their lines all mapped out." None of us thought to point out that we had no access to his intelligence while we were imprisoned.

After the pleasantries, the Colonel got to the point. "Europe is swamped with refugees right now. We haven't yet cleared the backlog from the war, and now the flow of eastern refugees is too much for most of the democratic nations to absorb all at once. I'm afraid you may have some difficulty getting accepted anywhere."

There was silence on our part. After all we had been through, we were not going to be discouraged this easily, but it was not welcome news. The Colonel continued. "After you're all cleared medically, I'll release you to the care of the refugee organizations. They enjoy privileged status in Germany, at least for the time being. But this being politics, I'd advise you to make your own best efforts to find a permanent home, wherever you can. Otherwise, you could lose your protections with the stroke of a bureaucrat's pen. I don't know what any future German government would do with you, after that."

Germany was in transition at that time. The Allies partitioned the country after the war, and the American, French and British Zones had been combined, but no governing structure was yet in place. We could not know what form it would take, and whether it would lean east or west. Having seen Czechoslovakia fall so easily, this gave us plenty of cause for concern. And it was not merely our harrowing experiences making us paranoid. The very rationale for the Marshall Plan was to rebuild the German nation in such a way as to make it resistant to communism, which was a real fear at the time.

"They wouldn't send us back, would they?" I asked.

The Colonel shrugged, as if he did not want to answer the question. After some time, he added, "I would hope not, but I don't know. I can't rule anything out."

After another week at the field hospital, we were transferred to US Military facilities near Regensburg. Some of us still had bandages, and my ankle was still in a cast. Along the way, we were stopped by a German internal security checkpoint. The officials came through and began to question us, and did not seem friendly. "How did you escape your border security?" they asked me, but before I could answer, our American escort interrupted with instructions. "Only give your name, and status as a refugee. They have no right to demand anything more." The German officials kept at it, questioning individuals who had just seen others being told not to answer, so we only answered with our name and status. This seemed to irritate the Germans, but the Americans were uncompromising, and appeared to be on solid legal ground. To me, it was fantastic to be able to rebuff an interrogation without fear of being beaten, or even executed. I think I began to smile at the frustrated Germans, making them grow even more incensed. After a while, it occurred to them that their efforts were futile, so they gave up and sent us along. But the Colonel's advice also came to mind. Germany was in transition, and there were plenty of communists at various levels, who would treat us as their enemies.

On our arrival at the US Military facilities near Regensburg, we were met by officers of various units, who separated us students from everyone else. They then took us to interrogation rooms, and questioned each of us separately. Most of the questions concerned how the Communist government dealt with students, and what sentences they handed out. They were also interested in the relationship between the pro-communist militia units and the communist government. Unlike any interrogation I had previously been through, I was never mistreated, and all my needs were attended to. Nonetheless, I experienced abiding anxiety at the interaction with those in power over me, and would carry this the rest of my life.

After the questioning was complete, the students were summoned to see the American commander. He notified us that the details of our escape, and the wounds we sustained, were fully documented, in the eventuality that those responsible could be put on trial. Then he gave us new documents, as we no longer had any of our own, and handed us back to the security officers. Those who were not students were sent to different places. I was aware that Jan and Borek, with their extensive knowledge of the Czechoslovak military, were sent directly to the USA. We students were allowed to recover fully, and after our casts were removed, they took us to Frankfurt, where we were accommodated at a facility for refugees.

The nightmares were worst after the initial shock of the events subsided. As my physical wounds healed, the psychological wounds called attention to themselves, as needs to be addressed. I spoke to my colleagues, who all recounted the same experiences. The escape in particular, where we saw three friends die gruesome deaths, was replaying itself in our dreams. Sometimes I imagined it being me getting torn up by dogs, while other times I awoke in a sweat, as I relived the horror of seeing everything with my own eyes. I don't think my conscious mind had yet accepted that what we experienced was real. Life was calm before, and it promised to be calm once again, so that experience was such an outlier, I came to regard it as just a bad dream. Then, in my actual dreams, I had to confront its reality.

To busy myself, I began to write detailed notes of everything that had transpired. I hoped one day, a broad audience could read for themselves what the communists did to their own people. And I also think this helped me come to terms with it all. But above all, I tried to stay busy, to avoid occasions where I would have too much time to think and reflect. I was surrounded by fellow students, and nearby was a small hotel where most of the exiled Czechoslovak politicians stayed for short periods of time. We secretly met with some of them, and they included some high level government officials, and senior military officers. All of them had been sentenced to hard labor in the uranium mines of Jáchymov. They were given priority in finding a permanent home, leaving the students as a problem for the officials.

After quite a bit of shuffling around, we ended up in Ludwigsburg, where most of the exiled Czechoslovak intelligentsia were housed. This reunited us with many familiar students and professors. They had all heard of our escape, and accepted us immediately. We spontaneously organized a Czechoslovak university in exile, which we called *Masaryk University*. We developed a curriculum, and quickly began course work. We lacked any formal accreditation, but we simply wanted to be busy doing something productive. Everyone was more than happy to participate.

Perhaps predictably, it did not last long. We were first given two years to wind down our operations, during which time we were expected to find permanent homes in democratic countries. Word circulated that their principal concern was that such a high concentration of Czechoslovak exiles in one place would invite communist infiltrators, posing as refugees. I always wondered what such infiltrators could report, that would not be obvious. Yes, we were deeply opposed to the regime that tried to kill us, and before that sentenced us to life in the uranium mines for supporting democracy. Surely they did not need infiltrators to tell them that. But security was a priority in post-war Germany, and we quickly picked up on the attitudes of the administrators. They were sympathetic to us and treated us well, but our numbers were a concern. Most other refugee camps in Germany had developed problems with violence, and they were under pressure to move people out.

At another meeting a short time later, they surprised us. "We'd like you to leave sooner than the two-year wind-down window we first spoke of."

"Where should we go?" was our question. There was no answer, since we were there because we were refugees, with no place to go. The officials in charge of us began to scramble, and submit paperwork as quickly as they were able. By late May, to satisfy the bureaucratic pressure they were facing, they came up with a plan for us. We were given permission to visit France for up to six weeks. This would give us time to visit various universities, and possibly find a place to study. If we failed to find anything, we could return to Ludwigsburg at the end of the six weeks. We had been together since our time as political prisoners, so we felt comfortable agreeing to the plan.

In all, we were Peter, Pavel, Frank, Michal, Cenek, Evžen, Bohumil and myself. We were each given a rucksack with a change of clothes, documentation, and two pairs of shoes. With that, we were off for France.

Chapter 9: Tour de France

We were given permission to spend six weeks in France, after which we had to return to Ludwigsburg, or lose our protected status as displaced persons. At the suggestion of the International Refugee Organization (IRO), we found a truck at a nearby market, and the owner agreed to take us to Strasbourg. His only condition was that we help him load and unload his cargo. We changed trucks in Strasbourg, and the driver agreed to take us to Paris, with the same conditions. A little labor as the price for transportation seemed like a good deal. The Italian driver even brought us some fresh French bread, a large circle of cheese, some salami, and two bottles of wine. He then showed us a room where we could sleep. In the morning, he brought us coffee and more food, and then we made for the Paris suburb of Brie-Comte.

We found ourselves in suburban Paris, not speaking the language, and unsure what we should do next. We looked around as though looking for something specific, and began to feel concerned that we were lost.

"They knew we were coming, right?" asked Cenek.

We all shrugged, and Michal said, "I'm pretty sure they did."

After only a few minutes of uncertainty, we were approached by two men calling for Pavel. They were from the British Embassy, and relatives of Pavel's in England had sponsored him, so he could emigrate to that country. Pavel left with them as they returned to the embassy, and they told us to stay where we were. Again, we felt alone, and wondered if someone was going to come for us. A few minutes later, we were approached by our friends Robert and Jurek, the two former Czechoslovak parliamentarians who had escaped with us. They were already established in Paris, and made some suggestions. They called two taxi cabs and took us directly to La Sorbonne. Evidently, the IRO had made some calls on our behalf.

After a short ride, we stopped outside the building with a sign in French and English, "seat of the University de Paris-La Sorbonne". We went inside, and our colleague Peter, who was proficient in the French Language, went to the information desk to make inquiries. We were pleasantly surprised that they too were expecting us. We were next introduced to a Professor Bertram, who called on several student leaders to answer all our questions. After extending every courtesy, the professor returned with two of his colleagues, whose task it was to break the news to us: only one student could be accepted at this time. Peter was the obvious choice, given his mastery of the French language. Of the eight of us who started out, two had found a new home, and we shared heartfelt goodbyes.

As if motivated by regret over not being able to accept the rest of us, Professor Bertram and two student leaders took us on a tour of Paris. We saw Notre Dame Cathedral, the Opera de Paris, and the old center of town, and eventually ended up at Saint Denis University, where we met two of Bertram's colleagues. After more pleasantries, they informed us they could take two students, if they spoke adequate French, which we did not. After that, Professor

Bertram took us to a cottage he owned, south of Paris. His family had arranged space for us to sleep, and fed us well.

In the morning, the professor sketched out a tentative plan on a map. We would travel around France, and check in on various institutions, to see if any one was willing to take any of us. He introduced us to his neighbor Henrique, who would take us in his farmer's truck for the next stage of our trip, to Orleans. He was pleased by our attempts at the French language, which were sufficient for casual conversation, if not for studies at top universities. Arriving in Orleans, Henrique gave us directions to local universities, and with good wishes, departed.

We stood around for a while, trying to get our bearings, until after about fifteen minutes we stopped a car to ask for directions. We soon found our destination, and already waiting for us was a Professor Venrieve, colleague of Professor Bertram. They stressed they could accept two students, provided they were proficient in French. Again, we were defeated by our inadequate mastery of French. After our meeting, Prof. Venrieve arranged for our group to meet two of his assistants, who were headed east to the town of Auxerre. They would be happy to give us a lift.

At this point, it should have been clear to the remaining six of us that we would not be accepted at a French university without a much stronger command of the French language than any of us possessed. And we should have returned to Ludwigsburg, and reported the results of our efforts. We were being passed from person to person, and each one went through the motions of trying to appear helpful in the face of obvious futility. But we continued to stick with the plan, like many who cling to irrational hope, because it was the only hope we had at that time.

The two assistants drove us to the east, through the Loire Valley, before stopping at a farm in Champignelles. The scenery was gorgeous, with valleys full of grapevines. It was close enough to looking like home that I became somewhat wistful, wishing history had turned out differently. The assistant named Jacques introduced us to his family, but then announced he would be staying there for a week. The second assistant, Julian, would take us on our next leg.

Julian drove us through a lot of unfamiliar farmland, and we lost our sense of where we were. He stopped at the home of a relative, and we sat down in a beautiful garden, full of flowers. Once we learned where we were, we objected that he had taken us too far to the south. He defended himself, saying he needed to, or we could have been shot by farmers guarding their fields from too many refugees, roaming the country. We knew he was motivated by his own interests, but that fear of the local farmers stuck with us. He sketched a route for us, and gave us the names of farmers who could provide transportation along the way.

We were quite upset by the turn of events. It was one thing to realize that our trip was probably futile. It was another to reach the end of the line, and be abandoned by the last link in the chain, who could find nobody else to pass us off to. We were now on foot, across France.

The land was full of vineyards, and to all appearances, was an idyllic place to be. Only we could be perceived as threats by farmers who were trying to re-stock their wine cellars after being pillaged by the Nazis during the war. Our food did not last long, and soon we were very hungry. A few days on foot, and we were willing to eat most anything. We found a wild bush with small round fruit, that tasted sweet. Not even knowing what it was, or if it was safe, we filled our bellies with it, and found it a satisfying meal.

Darkness was setting in when we found a very old wooden bridge, adorned with ornamental edges. Below was a small brook. Seeing no alternative, we settled in under the bridge for a night of uncomfortable sleep. I kept re-living the experiences of our escape, where we also had to sneak around the countryside, without a place to lay our heads. France was a peaceful country, so we did not have to fear being murdered by the authorities, but the farmers might not be so generous if they suspected us of poaching their grapes.

We walked a long way the following morning, before sitting down for a rest where a small river joined the Loire. A farmer was nearby and surprised us, but hearing us speaking in Czech, he extended his arm in a gesture of invitation to get in and ride with him. We gladly accepted, and rode with him for some distance. Checking the names of the villages against our map, we concluded we could make it to Dijon, if we kept on our current heading. The farmer finished his trip and let us go, again on foot. We slept under another bridge that night, and continued on foot the following day. We drank from the rivers we encountered, and were now very hungry. We had only eaten intermittently over the past week, and all the walking was beginning to take its toll.

Towards the end of the day, with hunger gnawing

at us, Evžen seemed to take interest in the grass growing near a river. He ripped up a large bundle, washed it in the river, then put a small wad in his mouth.

"You're not going to eat grass, are you?" I asked.

He looked at me with a mischievous expression, and said, "Ah, but zees is le grasse provençale," as if that made it some kind of gourmet dish. He ate his small wad of grass, and then some more. Seeing this, the rest of us began to eye that grass through the lens of our empty stomachs, and within about five minutes, all of us had at least partially filled our bellies with grass. People have since tried to explain to me that grass has no nutritional value, so it was a waste of effort. But none of them had ever been in the same situation, so their opinion is unconvincing. I know grass has no useful calories, but it may have certain vitamins and minerals that helped replenish our reserves. Because when we had no alternative, a meal of grass was better than nothing.

We crossed a river, and in a short time found ourselves in an open field next to a corn field. Looking around carefully, we noticed no farmers anywhere, and the field was in bloom with small blue flowers. We picked as many of the flowers as we could reasonably gather, collected some more grass, rinsed it in the river, and ate it all. After that, we walked a little longer, but fatigue was getting the better of us, and our stomachs were cramping. I'm not sure whether that was from eating the grass, or the germs in the streams we were drinking from, often near grazing cattle.

By late afternoon, we were feeling somewhat better, so we agreed to continue walking. After several more hours, we stopped to review our map, because we thought we should be near the town of St. Etienne. Out of nowhere, two men and a woman appeared behind us. They saw us reviewing our map, and heard our accents, and took pity on us. They invited us to their farm, but we politely declined, thinking we needed to make haste and return to Frankfurt. The woman left while the men remained with us, and she returned shortly with some fresh bread and cheese, which we ate ravenously. After eating, they warned us not to go to St. Etienne, where we might meet with a hostile reception, and suggested a more direct route to the south.

We continued another fifteen kilometers, before stopping at another bridge over the Loire, where we bathed and washed our clothes in the river. Nearby were wild berry bushes, so we ate as many as we could pick, and felt satisfied for the time being. We continued on until dark, until finally, we came to some broad-leafed trees and decided to sit down. We found a place under the trees, and fell asleep in sheer exhaustion.

We awoke early, spurred by the intense rays of sun poking through the trees. We followed the course of the river, and passed beautiful forests. But in spite of our positive encounters with those farmers we actually met, we still feared being shot as trespassers, whenever we were near a farm. In part it was because of the warnings we received, but I can't discount the importance of what we had been through in Czechoslovakia. Any uncertain encounter would trigger a level of anxiety in us that those who have not been through something equally traumatic cannot fully understand. And so, as we walked through some of the nicest parts of France, where most farmers were sympathetic and might even invite us for a meal, we were too afraid to make contact on our own. Instead, we went so far as to eat grass, by my recollection about six times. We finished that long day sleeping under another bridge, after again eating a meal of fresh grass.

We awoke next morning in some pain. Our stomachs were again cramping, and our legs and feet were excruciatingly sore. We were also tired, hungry, and disoriented. Our wills were weakened by hunger and fatigue, and we were no longer thinking clearly. Our discussions were illogical and disjointed, and we were powerless to correct ourselves. We were not aware of it at the time, but I am now certain we were close to total collapse at that point.

Suddenly, a farmer's truck stopped at the side of the road, right next to us. It was brand new, which was unusual in this part of the country, which had not yet recovered from the war. A tall man got out of the truck, and approached us. "Where are you heading?" he asked.

In a soft voice, not from timidity but from weakness, Zdenek answered: "east, or to Fusille, to make our connection". We started a brief conversation, telling him of our long walk, our exhaustion, and hunger. He introduced himself as Louis, and said he could take us anywhere, because he was very familiar with this part of France. In the course of our conversation, he said we were not far from the district of Marseille. "I wonder if there are any universities there," I said, still clinging to our original, if futile, goal.

"There certainly is. I'll take you there in my own car." Seeing no better prospects anywhere, we agreed to go with him.

Louis drove us through a number of very

attractive towns and villages, and we soon felt a sea breeze when we neared L'Estague. Louis stopped at a convenient place, where we had a view of the city of Marseille, which was a beautiful sight. "I take it you're hungry," he soon said.

We all nodded eagerly, and he continued. "No problem, I'll take you to a nice place. He continued to the outskirts of Marseille, and stopped at a very attractive garden restaurant, frequented by the locals. "I've arranged a private room for you all," he said, and led us down to a cellar dining room. The table had already been set with many fruits, breads, and all sorts of French and Mediterranean foods. Seeing more food in one place than we had seen in a long time, we were taken aback. At first hesitantly, we began to eat. But after the first few bites, the depth of our hunger came through, and we started to eat ravenously. Wine was flowing freely, and we ate, drank, and laughed. We mistakenly felt like we had somehow earned this after enduring hunger for so long, and we never questioned what motives Louis might have had.

I don't remember anything after dinner. We woke the following day with terrible headaches, and aches all over. It was not from too much wine; it was much worse. As we got our bearings, we realized we were in an entirely different place than the previous evening. And the sound that woke us was that of trumpets playing Les Marseilles. It all had a military feel to it. We looked out the oddly shaped windows, and saw a large square with five large barracks and three smaller buildings. Four officers were conducting drills with perhaps a hundred soldiers. This was a military garrison. All of a sudden, Louis' inexplicable generosity came into context. We had obviously been tricked, but for what purpose?

Later, a very tall, fully uniformed officer came to see us. He spoke in French. "As you should know by now, you're in the compound of the French Foreign Legion. Seeing our befuddled expressions, he looked through some papers he had with him, then switched to broken German. "I have papers for you to sign, confirming your membership in the Legion." Then he started to explain the advantages of joining the Legion. Angrily, we protested that we had been deceived, and demanded to be released.

He replied that, "It is out of the ordinary to release anyone from service, once they enter the compound."

"We have refugee status with the IRO," I protested. The others demanded our papers back, pointing out that we were required to return to Frankfurt soon. The officer left and we were left to wonder how we got ourselves into this. Later in the day, a sergeant came and ordered everybody out to the *exercise square*. The other soldiers forcibly put us into line, and ran us through the same drills we had earlier seen in our window. It was an hour of hard exercise, finishing with a run around the square and back to our room. We were very tired, and they gave us little food to eat. They put us through this same routine every day for four consecutive days, while our food rations were cut. In the morning, we were given a bowl of soup and two slices of bread, then nothing during the day, and in the evening, a few pieces of fruit. The effect was to weaken our resolve, and soon we were privately discussing whether it might be better to sign the papers, and join the Legion. I knew nothing about the French Foreign Legion, except that they fought overseas, on some poor nation's land, often against the interests of the locals. I knew that concept too well, and could never bring myself to join. Every day we were asked whether we were ready to sign, and every day, we objected that we had been deceived, and demanded to be returned to Frankfurt, where our deadline was fast approaching.

For six days, we complained at every opportunity, and finally locked our room, pretending to be sick. On the seventh day, a major in the Legion came to our room. He introduced himself as Filipe, and began to speak Czech, with a strong northern Moravian accent. He said, "You're at Caserne Viènot. You've been deceived."

"We've been saying that for the last week," I objected, angrily.

"The Legion should not have done this. Our High Command has reviewed your case, and you will be released."

An hour later, another officer came with our papers, and a certificate of release from the Legion. He instructed us to be ready to leave at exactly midnight, and left. *Why not let us go now?* I wondered, pointlessly. It was exactly at midnight that major Filipe returned in a dress uniform, accompanied by the other soldier he had sent to us. They led us through a narrow corridor, out an unmarked door, and to a Legion truck. The officer ordered us into the truck, and we left the complex, afraid but hopeful.

We arrived at IRO headquarters in Strasbourg several days later, and were subject to a lengthy investigation into what actually transpired, and why IRO protected refugees had been deceptively conscripted into the Foreign Legion. After more shuttling around between Strasbourg, Frankfurt, and Regensburg, we ended up back at the Czechoslovak settlement in Ludwigsburg, except without Pavel and Peter, who were in England and France, respectively. The rest of us had wasted our time, risked our freedom, and maybe our lives. We experienced prolonged hunger to the point that we concluded grass was a good meal, and saw the south of France under less than ideal circumstances. We would have been better not making the trip, but this was the unfortunate situation for refugees in 1949. There were too many refugees for the democratic countries absorb all at once.

Personally, I did not find that adventure particularly traumatic. Not when compared to what came before. I was with close friends the whole time, and nobody had actively tried to kill any of us. And that had become the new standard by which to judge the severity of a situation. I came to envy anyone who could consider the French tour anything resembling traumatic.

Epilogue

The pressure to settle all refugees continued to mount, and while the numbers were daunting, the democratic countries slowly came around. I was accepted by Canada in early 1950, and soon settled in the Toronto area. There was a small Czech community at the time, and it has grown much larger in the years since. I had arrived in a safe and friendly country that was committed to treating everyone fairly, regardless of their political leanings. But I was alone. I had grown very close to the friends I made during my time as a political prisoner, and cemented those friendships during our harrowing escape. But each of them had now gone to some other country, and we lost touch. Finding myself with too much time alone, I began to re-live my losses of years earlier. I never saw my father again, although I occasionally received a letter from him. I would struggle with these wounds for some time, before experiencing true healing.

On my arrival in Canada, I had no money, I did not speak English, and my education was not documented. I went to a government-sponsored service that matched people to available jobs, and was assigned to an older gentleman, named Jack. He took an interest in my case, and worked with me for some time, but the initial interaction must have made him wonder what he had gotten himself into.

"What are your skills?"

"I'm familiar with pulsed-Doppler radar systems."

"You're an engineer?"

I did my best to explain my hobbled-together

education, and that I had no documents proving anything. I could hardly contact the communist regime and expect them to graciously provide everything I needed. Jack promised he would look into what measures we could take to obtain recognition of my education. In the meantime, I needed work, so he asked, "What else can you do?"

"I'm good at sports."

"How competitive?"

"I was a competitive boxer in the military. And I played hockey in the top Czechoslovak league."

And so my first job in Canada was as a boxer. I was paid $50 apiece for my first several fights, and won each of them. I was then offered $200 per fight to box at a higher level. I even won a few fights at that level, but when I woke up after being knocked out in my fourth fight, the doctor explained that I was done as a boxer. Back to see Jack at the employment agency.

Jack had not yet obtained an answer about recognizing my education, but he connected me with the Toronto Argos rowing club, where I did quite well. He also found me a part-time job with the Massey-Harris agricultural equipment company (it later became Massey-Ferguson), where I helped in the design of combines.

Then fall came, and Jack called me back to the employment office. When I arrived, he introduced me to a Mr. Wasserman, President of the Sudbury Wolves Senior A hockey team. He told me he could offer room and board, and a small stipend, but first I would have to try out by playing in several pre-season exhibition games. I was buying time, because I could never raise my game to a level that would pay a real salary, and I knew I would not be able to do this indefinitely. The pace of the Senior A game was well within my abilities, but the physicality was on another level entirely. That reality hit me in the second period of my second game, when I went into a corner and took a hard body check at an awkward angle, breaking my leg.

My spirits hit another bottom after that. I was in the hospital, and the team would pay my medical expenses, but I was done in competitive hockey, and had run out of skills to fall back on. After all I had been through, I always had hope for the future; that something would work out. But now, in a wealthy country, I had exhausted my options, and had no idea how I would establish myself.

That was when I was paid a visit by Jack from the employment agency, accompanied by an official from the University of Ottawa, who was also affiliated with the government. The solution to getting my education recognized was to get me acceptance into a Master's program, which would establish my qualifications, once complete. I was admitted to the University of Ottawa, where I focused on learning everything that was known about Doppler Radar. I also got a part-time job doing maintenance for a mining company, which kept me clothed and fed while I studied. At the end of my studies, my advisor in Ottawa put me in touch with a major defense corporation that had been developing electronic security measures in the north of Canada. Then after about two years of work in the Ottawa area, I was asked about my interest in a special project. They had been tasked with deploying a comprehensive radar system across the far north of Canada, to be jointly administered with the United States, which would provide an early warning of approaching

Soviet nuclear bombers.

I met with those in charge, and explained how I thought conventional radar could be improved. My ideas happened to correspond to what they were already intending to do, so they made me an offer. It would take several years to complete the project, during which time the engineering teams would have to live in the high arctic. I accepted on the spot, as I was more than happy to build a system to guard against a Soviet nuclear attack.

I soon departed for the boreal forests of northern Saskatchewan, where the preliminary work would begin. We were in the region of Lake Athabasca, and were accompanied by several Dené and Inuit people, who would help us adjust to our environment throughout the project. Then there came a delay, and the workers were told they could go home to their families, until logistics could be worked out. I was struck on the spot by the fact that I was the only one who had no family to go to. That was my last major low point, and I think it showed. One of our guides, who we called Rudi, turned to me and said, "Come with me. I'll teach you about the wilderness."

We made our way to the area around Hay River, on the southern shore of Great Slave Lake. There were insects everywhere, but Rudi made some herbal extracts we applied to our hair and clothing, and they did not bother us. It was only then that I finally realized how vast true wilderness can be. The few pockets of wilderness back in Moravia now paled in comparison.

On the second day of our trek through the forest, I said, "Rudi, at first I thought I must be dreaming, but now I'm sure it's true. There are people in the forest, watching us."

Rudi smiled, and said, "It's the Tlicho. They've been treated badly by settlers, so they're leery of strangers."

I was suddenly a little nervous. I had no idea how I would react if expected to answer for the wrongs of settlers in a conflict I didn't understand.

"Don't worry," he assured me, as he saw my reaction. I settled down a little, and soon came to revel in the sheer scale of the forest. The other thing that struck me was how peaceful it was. There were dangers, and Rudi was there to alert me to them. But I found a sense of my place in the world there, in those boreal forests.

Suddenly, Rudi snapped at me to remain still. I had not noticed anything, but he went off alone. He returned with two Dené-Chipewyan men in traditional native clothing. After a brief introduction, he turned to me and said, "They've agreed to welcome us to their village."

We came to the village, where they had horses, livestock, and many teepees, made from animal skins. We were taken to the chief, where Rudi conversed for some time, often gesturing towards me. Finally, the chief raised his left hand towards me, which I understood as a formal welcome to his tribe.

In the ensuing days, I learned to make teepees, to fish with only traditional implements, to ride a horse while throwing a spear, which I only managed to my right, not my left. Then they had a ceremony for me, where ceremonial smoke was directed to my face, and the chief put both his hands on my shoulders, while speaking his native language. Afterwards, Rudi told me, "You're now a member of the Dené-Chipewyan tribe. They don't often do this for white men, but they say you have a good heart."

I enjoyed about three weeks with the Dené-Chipewyan tribe, and felt more refreshed than I had in years. Those people lived their lives true to their traditions, even more than we had in Moravia. Their acceptance of me into their tribe filled a void in my heart created when I was cut off from my own traditions.

The project soon resumed, and we moved to the high arctic, where we spent several years among the Inuit. We built a series of radar installations across the whole breadth of Canada's far north, that came to be known as the Distant Early Warning Line, or DEW Line. Each installation had to be built on permafrost, and ships could only deliver materials during the summer months. The rest of the time was spent setting up, tuning and calibrating the radar installations, which was my specialty. The Inuit also befriended me, and I learned to live like them in every way. One night as I was feeling one of my bouts of sadness and loneliness, I went outside, and raised my head to the most spectacular display of northern lights I could ever imagine seeing. I was so bowled over by the beauty that I thanked God for making it, and for allowing me to see it, which could never have happened if I had not moved half way across the world. And I never would have moved half way across the world if I had not been forced to. That was the moment where I felt I had truly healed from the grief of my losses. I continued to remember my youth, and I still get sad over the loss of people I loved, but after that it became something I knew I could live with.

We finished the DEW line in 1957, after which they took us to the beautiful city of Vancouver. I received a letter of commendation from Prime

Minister Diefenbaker, and a check for wages awarded for the whole duration of the project. It was enough for me to build a house in Vancouver, where I obtained my doctorate. With my qualifications established, and experience successfully completing such a high profile project, many doors opened for me. I later moved back to Toronto, where I married, taught at the University of Toronto, and worked on many challenging engineering projects over the course of a long, satisfying career.

I don't know with certainty how most of my colleagues ended up, but I think they probably did alright. After what we lived through, I think we all learned to take nothing for granted. My friend Jarda Drobný defected in 1949 and reached the pinnacle of the tennis world, twice winning at Roland Garros, and finally achieved his dream of winning at Wimbledon, in 1954. He settled in England with a wife and daughter, but I never saw him again.

Communism in Czechoslovakia lasted 41 years. The first decade was the most repressive, and can rightly be considered a reign of terror. Things began to relax a little after that, to the point where an echo of the Czechoslovak tradition of liberal government poked up above the surface in 1968. It was swiftly crushed by a Soviet military occupation, and a second repressive period followed. But it was not as brutal, or as long, as communism had begun to lose its convictions. The last communist government fell in 1989, and the nation returned to democratic rule. Masaryk's dream of a united Czechoslovakia died soon afterwards, as the Slovak people voted to become an independent nation. But the split happened in an entirely peaceful manner, and the two countries enjoy friendly relations to this day.

I don't like to lecture young people about what we went through, as every generation faces its own challenges. I only urge everyone to be vigilant in defending their free institutions. As I know too well, the consequences of their loss can be quite serious.

###

Addendum: Czech Pronunciation. Some tips on pronouncing Czech words. *R* makes a hard sound, and both *w* and *v* make the *v* sound in Czech. Every letter is spoken in Czech, so words can be easily sounded out, but unlike English, two-letter combinations rarely specify a single sound. Instead, letters are modified with various accent marks, to modify their pronunciation. To modify *s* to the equivalent of *sh*, the Czech character is *š*. Similarly, *ch* is *č*, and *zh* is *ž*. Czech has a unique sound, specified as *ř*, that is often pronounced *rzh*, but sounds much harsher, like a badly tuned car engine. An *e* modified to *ě* changes it from *eh* to *yeh*. An *á*, makes a sound like *aaah*, such as what a doctor tells you to say. An *í* makes the sound eeee. The letter *ů* is pronounced *oooh*. *Ch* is the same in Czech and German, and sounds like someone needs to clear their throat. A *c* is always soft, as in *ts*, never pronounced like a *k*. And the letter *j* is never pronounced like a *g*. It's always soft, like a *y*.